Ninja Foodi XL Pro Air Oven Cookbook

115 Quick, Delicious & Easy-to-Prepare Recipes to Air Fry, Bake, and Roast for Your Family

Monte Wood

© **Copyright 2020 - All rights reserved.**

The content contained within this book may not be reproduced, duplicated or transmitted without direct written permission from the author or the publisher.

Under no circumstances will any blame or legal responsibility be held against the publisher, or author, for any damages, reparation, or monetary loss due to the information contained within this book, either directly or indirectly.

Legal Notice:

This book is copyright protected. It is only for personal use. You cannot amend, distribute, sell, use, quote or paraphrase any part, or the content within this book, without the consent of the author or publisher.

Disclaimer Notice:

Please note the information contained within this document is for educational and entertainment purposes only. All effort has been executed to present accurate, up to date, reliable, complete information. No warranties of any kind are declared or implied. Readers acknowledge that the author is not engaged in the rendering of legal, financial, medical or professional advice. The content within this book has been derived from various sources. Please consult a licensed professional before attempting any techniques outlined in this book.

By reading this document, the reader agrees that under no circumstances is the author responsible for any losses, direct or indirect, that are incurred as a result of the use of the information contained within this document, including, but not limited to, errors, omissions, or inaccuracies.

Contents

Introduction 5

Ninja Foodi XL Pro Air Fry Oven 6

   Quick User Guide 6

Chapter One: Breakfast Recipes 8

   French Toast Sticks 8

   Pizza Rolls 9

   Ham and Cheese Scones 10

   Raisin Muffins 11

   Blueberry-Lemon Scones 12

   Banana Bread 13

   Puffed Egg Tarts 14

   Mushrooms Frittata 15

   Pumpkin Muffins 16

Chapter Two: Snacks and Appetizer Recipes 17

   Carrot Chips 17

   Pasta Chips 18

   Egg Rolls 19

   Avocado Fries 20

   Ranch Kale Chips 21

   Cheese Sticks 22

   Plantains Chips 23

   Buffalo Cauliflower 24

   Potato Fries 25

   Sweet Potato Tots 26

   Sweet Potato Chips 27

   Onion Rings 28

Chapter Three: Poultry Recipes 29

   Panko Chicken Breast 29

   Maple Chicken Thighs 30

   Chicken Bake 31

   Crumbed Tenderloins 32

   Chicken Schnitzel 33

   Sesame Chicken Thighs 34

   Baked Butter Thighs 35

   Primavera Chicken 36

   Chicken Meatballs 37

Chapter Four: Beef, Pork, and Lamb 38

   Lamb Leg with Mint Sauce 38

   Roast Lamb with Potatoes 39

   Lamb Chops with Garlic Sauce 40

   Breaded Pork Chops 41

   Pork Chops with Broccoli 42

   Garlicky Pork Chops 43

   Spiced Pork Chops 44

   Russian Beef 45

Beef Potato Medley 46

Chapter Five: Seafood Recipes 47

Baked Shrimp with Garlic Sauce............ 47

Haddock Cream Casserole 48

Halibut Scallops Bake 49

Dill Seafood Paella 50

Lobster Tail Casserole 51

Breaded Shrimp 52

Garlic Parmesan Shrimp 53

White Fish with Lemon Pepper 54

Seafood Mushrooms Casserole 55

Chapter Six: Vegetables and Sides 56

Italian Baked Vegetables 56

Vegetable Casserole 57

Sweet Potato Casserole 58

Brussels Sprouts Gratin 59

Green Bean Casserole 60

Mayo Broccoli Casserole 61

Cauliflower Broccoli Medley 62

Vegetables Mix 63

Mushroom Skewers 64

Chapter Seven: Entertaining Recipes 65

Chicken Sheet Bake................................... 65

Chicken Enchiladas 66

Roasted Chicken.. 67

Whole Turkey with Gravy 68

Turkey breast... 69

Baked Potatoes.. 70

Air Fried Pizza.. 71

Blooming Onion 72

Thanksgiving Turkey 74

Chicken Casserole 75

Fiesta Chicken Casserole.......................... 76

Hash brown casserole............................... 77

Meatball Casserole 78

Ground Beef Casserole............................. 79

Chapter Eight: Dessert Recipes............80

Pear Pies.. 80

Chocolate Cake.. 81

Apple Pies.. 82

Cherry Crumble 83

Butter Cake.. 84

Cherry Eggrolls.. 85

Pecan Apples... 86

Fudgy Brownies 87

Strawberry Roll Cake................................. 88

Conclusion..89

Introduction

This is the age of single pot cooking where digitally controlled kitchen appliances are designed with several cooking modes to cook a variety of meals in no time. Today, finding a multipurpose cooking unit is not that of a challenge; rather, finding a perfect one for your kitchen requires a bit of a struggle, as there are unlimited options available. One brand that has earned our confidence in this regard is Ninja Foodi. Not only has the brand launched series of cooking appliances, but it keeps raising the bars by bringing new ideas to the market. The Ninja Foodi XL pro Air Fry Oven is one such innovation that has taken over the food-tech world with its amazing cooking features, a smart design, the XL size, and a multilayer cooking system.

This 10-in-1 multipurpose kitchen miracle is capable of providing a variety of cooking options all in a single device. With its efficient electric heating system, now you can bake, roast, Air fry, broil and dehydrate all types of food in no time. The user-friendly control system and its multifunctional heating mechanism make this appliance cost and time effective. If you are a foodie and love to cook a variety of meals for you and your family, then Ninja Foodi XL Pro Air Fry Oven is the right fit for you.

Before Ninja Foodi XL Air Fry Oven, cooking large portions of food in a single cooking session was really a problem for me. I had to cook in batches, which was quite time-consuming. But the Ninja Foodi XL pro Air Fry Oven has put an end to such problems; whether it's roasting full-size chicken or turkey, I can cook them easily using its WHOLE ROAST function. It can Roast, Bake, Air Fry, Toast, cook Pizza, Reheat, Broil and Dehydrate food in any of its four racks. The good news is that with the help of the recipe collection shared in this cookbook, you can create a complete menu in your Ninja Foodi XL Pro.

Ninja Foodi XL Pro Air Fry Oven

After the successful launch of its series of Air Fryer and Air Fry Ovens, Ninja Foodi has come up with its XL Pro Air Fry Oven to meet the needs of those who want to cook large servings sizes, whole turkeys, or chicken in their electric oven while trying different modes of cooking at one place. When we unbox the Ninja XL Air Fry Oven, the following are the accessories that are found along with the basic oven unit:

- Main Ninja XL Air Fry Oven
- Air fry basket
- Roast tray
- Sheet pan
- 2 wire racks
- Removable crumb tray

Air Fry Oven's Specifications:

A Ninja XL Air Fry Oven comes with the following unit specifications. All users are suggested to look into these features before bringing the unit home:

- Capacity: 12 lbs
- Dimensions in: 17.09L x 20.22W x 13.34H
- Power supply: 120V – 60Hz
- Maximum Draw: 1800 Watts

The control panel is present on the front-top portion of the oven with a glass door below it. Inside the oven, there are four layers to adjust your food. You can select "RACK LEVEL" from 1-4 after placing the food in a particular layer. Then the function key is used to select the cooking functions. The temperature and time keys are used to increase or decrease the values, and the same keys are used to set the darkness and slices of the toasts and bagels when their respective modes are selected. Once everything is set, the START and PAUSE button is used to initiate preheating and cooking.

Quick User Guide

If you are a newbie or you are setting your hands on this appliance for the first time, then here is how you can cook using its different cooking functions:

1. First, plug in the Ninja Foodi XL pro Air Fry Oven and switch it ON. The led display will be lit up, indicating that the device is working.
2. Since this Ninja XL pro Air Fry Oven quickly preheats, you need to prepare the food first and keep it ready for cooking before preheating.
3. Place the Drip or crumb tray inside, at the bottom of the oven to protect its base from food particle and grease.
4. Use the Air fryer basket, baking pan, roasting pan, or any other suitable accessory to place the food inside according to the instructions of a particular recipe.
5. You can insert trays into any portion of this air fry oven to accommodate your food in four layers if needed and select the RACK LAYER option 1,2,3,4 from the control panel according to your need.
6. When the food is ready, you can preheat the appliance. Close its door and select the desired cooking operation: Bake, Whole roast, Air Roast, Air Broil, Air Fry, Dehydrate, pizza, toast, bagel, or Reheat.
7. By selecting this program, the device will show the preset temperature and cooking time on the display; you can change it by using the "+" or "- "keys for temperature and time to increase or decrease the values, respectively.
8. If you are toasting bread or bagels, then use the temp and time keys to adjust the desired darkness of the toasts and the number of slices. The machine will automatically adjust the cooking temperature and time according to the desired darkness and set slices.
9. Press the start button to initiate preheating. The display timer does not start ticking until the appliance is preheated. When it reaches the desired temperature, the display will show "FOOD" and beep to show if the device is preheated.
10. Place the prepared food inside and close the lid to initiate cooking.
11. Once the cooking function is completed, the device will beep to indicate that the food is now ready to serve.

Chapter One: Breakfast Recipes

French Toast Sticks

Prep Time: 15 minutes.
Cook Time: 8 minutes.
Serves: 6

Ingredients:

- 12 slices Texas toast
- 1 cup milk
- 5 large eggs
- 4 tablespoons butter, melted
- 1 teaspoon vanilla extract
- 1/4 cup granulated sugar
- 1 tablespoon cinnamon
- Maple syrup, to serve

Preparation:

1. Slice each bread slice into three breadsticks.
2. Beat eggs with butter, vanilla, and milk in a mixing bowl until fully incorporated.
3. Whisk sugar with cinnamon in a separate bowl.
4. Dip the egg-milk mixture and place them on the steel rack of the Ninja XL Pro Air Fry Oven.
5. Place the steel rack over the cooking pan of the Ninja XL Pro Air Fry Oven.
6. Drizzle the cinnamon sugar over the breadsticks.
7. Select the "Air Fry" Mode using the Function Keys and select Rack Level 2.
8. Set its cooking time to 8 minutes and temperature to 350 degrees F then press "START/STOP" to initiate preheating.
9. Place the breadsticks in the cooking pan inside the Ninja XL Pro Air Fry Oven.
10. Close its door and allow the toasts to cook.
11. Once done, serve with maple syrup on top.

Serving Suggestion: Serve the toast sticks with chocolate syrup.

Variation Tip: Use honey for mildly sweet taste.

Nutritional Information Per Serving:
Calories 284 | Fat 7.9g | Sodium 704mg | Carbs 46g | Fiber 3.6g | Sugar 6g | Protein 18g

Pizza Rolls

Prep Time: 15 minutes.

Cook Time: 12 minutes.

Serves: 6

Ingredients:

- 1 ready-rolled puff pastry, thawed
- 1 teaspoon dried oregano
- 6 tablespoons pasta sauce
- 3 ½ ounces wafer thin ham
- 3 ½ ounces mature cheddar, grated
- 1 egg, beaten

Preparation:

1. Spread the puff pastry on the working surface into a rectangle.
2. Add pasta sauce on top, and spread it evenly.
3. Place ham slices on the sauce, drizzle oregano, and cheese on top.
4. Roll the puff pastry and slice this roll into 2 inches thick pinwheels.
5. Place the pizza rolls in the baking pan and brush them with egg.
6. Select the "Bake" Mode using the Function Keys and select Rack Level 2.
7. Set its cooking time to 12 minutes and temperature to 390 degrees F then press "START/STOP" to initiate preheating.
8. Once preheated, place the pizza rolls in the Ninja Foodi XL Pro Air Fryer Oven.
9. Serve fresh.

Serving Suggestion: Serve the pizza rolls with a cheese dip and crumbled crispy bacon on top.

Variation Tip: Add sliced olives or pepperoni to the filling for a change of flavors.

Nutritional Information Per Serving:

Calories 214 | Fat 5.1g |Sodium 231mg | Carbs 31g | Fiber 5g | Sugar 2.1g | Protein 17g

Ham and Cheese Scones

Prep Time: 15 minutes.
Cook Time: 25 minutes.
Serves: 6

Ingredients:

- 2 cups all-purpose flour
- 1 tablespoon baking powder
- 2 teaspoons sugar
- 1 teaspoon salt
- 2 tablespoons butter, cubed
- 1 cup ham, diced, cooked
- ¼ cup scallion, chopped
- 4 ounces cheddar cheese, shredded
- ¼ cup milk
- ¾ cup heavy cream

Preparation:

1. Whisk baking powder with flour, sugar, salt, and butter in a mixing bowl.
2. Beat milk, cream, and all other ingredients in another bowl.
3. Stir in the flour-butter mixture and mix well until it forms a smooth dough.
4. Place this scones dough on a floured surface and spread it into a 7-inch round sheet.
5. Cut this dough sheet into 6 wedges of equal size.
6. Place these wedges in the cooking pan, lined with parchment paper.
7. Select the "Bake" Mode using the Function Keys and select Rack Level 2.
8. Set its cooking time to 25 minutes and temperature to 400 degrees F then press "START/STOP" to initiate preheating.
9. Once the Ninja Air Fryer oven is preheated, place the dough wedges in the Air Fry Oven.
10. When baked, serve the scones with morning eggs.

Serving Suggestion: Serve the scone with softened butter.

Variation Tip: Ham can be replaced with crumbled bacon as well.

Nutritional Information Per Serving:
Calories 387 | Fat 6g |Sodium 154mg | Carbs 37.4g | Fiber 2.9g | Sugar 15g | Protein 15g

Raisin Muffins

Prep Time: 15 minutes.
Cook Time: 18 minutes.
Serves: 12

Ingredients:

- 1 cup wheat bran
- 1 cup boiling water
- 4 ounces Greek yogurt
- 2 large eggs
- 1 ½ cup whole wheat flour
- 5 ½ ounces all-purpose flour
- ¾ cup of sugar
- ½ ounces ground cinnamon
- 2 teaspoons baking powder
- 3/4 teaspoons salt
- 1/4 teaspoon baking soda
- 1/8 teaspoons grated nutmeg
- 6 ounces butter
- 1 cup golden raisins
- 3/4 ounces flaxseed

Preparation:

1. Mix wheat bran with boiling water in a bowl and leave it for 5 minutes.
2. Add eggs, wheat flour, sugar, Greek yogurt, cinnamon, salt, baking soda, baking powder, butter, and nutmeg into the wheat bran, then mix well in a mixer.
3. Stir in raisins and mix the batter gently.
4. Divide this bran muffin batter into 12 greased muffin cups.
5. Select the "Bake" Mode using the Function Keys and select Rack Level 2.
6. Set its cooking time to 18 minutes and temperature to 400 degrees F then press "START/STOP" to initiate preheating.
7. Place the muffin cups in the Ninja XL Pro Air Fry Oven and close the door.
8. Serve fresh.

Serving Suggestion: Serve the muffins with chocolate syrup on top.
Variation Tip: Add mixed nuts to the batter.
Nutritional Information Per Serving:
Calories 212 | Fat 12g |Sodium 321mg | Carbs 4.4g | Fiber 4.4g | Sugar 8g | Protein 17.3g

Blueberry-Lemon Scones

Prep Time: 15 minutes.
Cook Time: 25 minutes.
Serves: 6

Ingredients:

- 2 cups all-purpose flour
- 1 tablespoon baking powder
- 2 teaspoons sugar
- 1 teaspoon salt
- 2 ounces of coconut oil
- 1 cup fresh blueberries
- ¼ ounces lemon zest
- 8 ounces of coconut milk

Preparation:

1. Blend coconut oil with salt, sugar, baking powder, and flour in a food processor.
2. Transfer this flour mixture to a mixing bowl.
3. Now add coconut milk and lemon zest to the flour mixture, then mix well.
4. Fold in blueberries and mix the dough well until smooth.
5. Spread this blueberry dough into a 7-inch round and place it in a pan.
6. Refrigerate the blueberry dough for 15 minutes, then slice it into 6 wedges.
7. Layer the cooking pan Ninja XL Pro Air Fry Oven with a parchment sheet.
8. Place the blueberry wedges in the lined cooking pan.
9. Select the "Bake" Mode using the Function Keys and select Rack Level 2.
10. Set its cooking time to 25 minutes and temperature to 400 degrees F then press "START/STOP" to initiate preheating.
11. Once preheated, place the blueberry wedges in the Air Fry Oven and close its door to cook.
12. Serve fresh.

Serving Suggestion: Serve the scones with sugar topping.

Variation Tip: replace blueberry with cranberry for change of flavors.

Nutritional Information Per Serving:
Calories 412 | Fat 25g |Sodium 132mg | Carbs 44g | Fiber 3.9g | Sugar 3g | Protein 18.9g

Banana Bread

Prep Time: 15 minutes.
Cook Time: 25 minutes.
Serves: 6

Ingredients:

- 4 bananas, peeled and sliced
- ¼ cup Greek yogurt
- 2 large eggs
- ½ ounce vanilla extract
- 10 ounces all-purpose flour
- ¾ cup of sugar
- 3 ounces oat flour
- 1 teaspoon baking powder
- 1 teaspoon baking soda
- 3/4 teaspoons salt
- 3/4 teaspoons ground cinnamon
- 1/2 teaspoon ground cloves
- 1/4 teaspoon ground nutmeg
- 3/4 cup coconut oil
- 1 cup toasted pecan

Preparation:

1. Layer a 10.5 x 5.5 inches loaf pan with a parchment sheet and keep it aside.
2. Mash the banana in a suitable bowl and add eggs, vanilla, and Greek yogurt, then mix well.
3. Cover this banana yogurt mixture and leave it for 30 minutes.
4. Meanwhile, mix cinnamon, flour, sugar, baking powder, oat flour, salt, baking soda, coconut oil, cloves, and nutmeg in a mixer.
5. Now slowly add banana mash mixture to the flour and continue mixing until smooth.
6. Fold in nuts and mix gently until evenly incorporated.
7. Spread this banana-nut batter in the prepared loaf pan.
8. Select the "Bake" Mode using the Function Keys and select Rack Level 2.
9. Set its cooking time to 25 minutes and temperature to 350 degrees F then press "START/STOP" to initiate preheating.
10. Once the Air Fry Oven is preheated, place the loaf pan in the oven and close its door to bake.
11. Slice and serve.

Serving Suggestion: Serve the bread slices with eggs and crispy bacon.
Variation Tip: Add chopped walnuts to the batter.
Nutritional Information Per Serving:
Calories 331 | Fat 2.5g | Sodium 595mg | Carbs 69g | Fiber 12g | Sugar 12g | Protein 8.7g

Puffed Egg Tarts

Prep Time: 15 minutes.
Cook Time: 21 minutes.
Serves: 4

Ingredients:

- 3/4 cup Cheddar cheese, shredded
- 4 large eggs
- ½ (17-oz package) frozen puff pastry, thawed
- 1 tablespoon fresh parsley, minced

Preparation:

1. Spread the pastry sheet on a floured surface and cut it into 4 squares of equal size.
2. Place the four squares in the air frying sheet of the Ninja XL Pro Air Fry Oven.
3. Select the "Air Fry" Mode using the Function Keys and select Rack Level 2.
4. Set its cooking time to 10 minutes and temperature to 300 degrees F then press "START/STOP" to initiate preheating.
5. Once preheated, place the Air Fryer basket inside the Air Fry Oven and close its door to cook.
6. Press the center of each pastry square using the back of a metal spoon,
7. Divide cheese into these indentations and crack one egg into each pastry.
8. Return the puffed tarts to the Air Fry Oven and close its door.
9. Select the "Air Fry" Mode using the Function Keys and select Rack Level 2.
10. Set its cooking time to 11 minutes and temperature to 350 degrees F then press "START/STOP" to initiate preheating.
11. Garnish the squares with parsley.
12. Serve warm.

Serving Suggestion: Serve the tarts with crispy bacon slices.

Variation Tip: Top egg with fresh herbs or chopped bell pepper.

Nutritional Information Per Serving:
Calories 197 | Fat 15g | Sodium 202mg | Carbs 58.5g | Fiber 4g | Sugar 1g | Protein 7.3g

Mushrooms Frittata

Prep Time: 15 minutes.
Cook Time: 15 minutes.
Serves: 6

Ingredients:

- 1 cup egg whites
- 2 tablespoons skim milk
- ¼ cup tomato, sliced
- ¼ cup mushrooms, sliced
- 2 tablespoons fresh chives, chopped
- Black pepper, to taste

Preparation:

1. Beat egg whites with mushrooms and the rest of the ingredients in a bowl.
2. Spread this egg white's mixture in a suitable casserole dish.
3. Place this casserole dish in the Ninja XL Pro Air Fry Oven and close its door.
4. Select the "Air Fry" Mode using the Function Keys and select Rack Level 2.
5. Set its cooking time to 15 minutes and temperature to 320 degrees F then press "START/STOP" to initiate preheating.
6. Slice and serve warm.

Serving Suggestion: Serve the frittata with toasted bread slices.

Variation Tip: Ground chicken can also be added to the frittata

Nutritional Information Per Serving:
Calories 138 | Fat 9.7g |Sodium 245mg | Carbs 32.5g | Fiber 0.3g | Sugar 2g | Protein 10.3g

Pumpkin Muffins

Prep Time: 15 minutes.
Cook Time: 15 minutes.
Serves: 6

Ingredients:

- 1 cup pumpkin puree
- 2 cups oats
- ½ cup honey
- 2 medium eggs beaten
- 1 teaspoon coconut butter
- 1 tablespoon cocoa nibs
- 1 tablespoon vanilla essence
- 1 teaspoon nutmeg

Preparation:

1. Whisk pumpkin puree with remaining ingredients in a mixer until smooth.
2. Divide this pumpkin oat batter into 12 muffin cups of a muffin tray.
3. Place this muffin tray in the Ninja XL Pro Air Fry Oven.
4. Select the "Air Fry" Mode using the Function Keys and select Rack Level 2.
5. Set its cooking time to 15 minutes and temperature to 360 degrees F then press "START/STOP" to initiate preheating.
6. Serve fresh.

Serving Suggestion: Serve the casserole with toasted bread slices.

Variation Tip: Add chopped nuts or chocolate chips to the batter.

Nutritional Information Per Serving:

Calories 391 | Fat 2.8g | Sodium 62mg | Carbs 37g | Fiber 9.2g | Sugar 5g | Protein 6.6g

Chapter Two: Snacks and Appetizer Recipes

Carrot Chips

Prep Time: 15 minutes.
Cook Time: 15 minutes.
Serves: 6

Ingredients:

- 2 lbs. carrots, sliced
- 1/4 cup olive oil
- 1 tablespoon of sea salt
- 1 teaspoon ground cumin
- 1 teaspoon ground cinnamon

Preparation:

1. Toss the carrot slices with oil, cumin, and cinnamon in a large bowl.
2. Grease the Ninja baking sheet and spread the carrot slices on it.
3. Transfer the baking sheet to the Air Fry Oven and Close its door.
4. Select the "Bake" Mode using the Function Keys and select Rack Level 2.
5. Set its cooking time to 15 minutes and temperature to 380 degrees F then press "START/STOP" to initiate preheating.
6. Flip the chips after 7-8 minutes and resume cooking.
7. Serve fresh.

Serving Suggestion: Serve the chips with tomato ketchup.

Variation Tip: Add paprika for more spice.

Nutritional Information Per Serving:
Calories 148 | Fat 22g | Sodium 350mg | Carbs 32.2g | Fiber 0.7g | Sugar 1g | Protein 4.3g

Pasta Chips

Prep Time: 15 minutes.
Cook Time: 20 minutes.
Serves: 4

Ingredients:

- ½ tablespoons olive oil
- ½ tablespoons nutritional yeast
- 1 cup bow tie pasta
- 2/3 teaspoons Italian Seasoning Blend
- 1/4 teaspoon salt

Preparation:

1. Cook and boil the pasta in salted water in half of the time as stated on the box, then drain it.
2. Toss the boiled pasta with salt, Italian seasoning, nutritional yeast, and olive oil in a bowl.
3. Spread this pasta in the Air Fryer basket evenly.
4. Transfer the pasta to the Air Fry Oven and Close its door.
5. Select the "Air Fry" Mode using the Function Keys and select Rack Level 2.
6. Set its cooking time to 5 minutes and temperature to 390 degrees F then press "START/STOP" to initiate preheating.
7. Toss the pasta and continue air frying for another 5 minutes.
8. Enjoy.

Serving Suggestion: Serve the chips with tomato ketchup.

Variation Tip: Drizzle parmesan on top before baking.

Nutritional Information Per Serving:

Calories 145 | Fat 6g | Sodium 412mg | Carbs 26g | Fiber 0.1g | Sugar 0.1g | Protein 3.5g

Egg Rolls

Prep Time: 15 minutes.

Cook Time: 14 minutes.

Serves: 6

Ingredients:

- 1 pound ground pork
- 1 tablespoon olive oil
- 1 tablespoon ginger, grated
- 1 garlic clove, minced
- 12 egg roll wrappers
- 1 teaspoon onion powder
- 1/4 teaspoon Chinese 5 spice
- 1 tablespoon soy sauce
- 2 ½ cups packaged fresh coleslaw

Preparation:

1. Saute pork with olive oil, ginger, garlic, onion powder, Chinese 5 spiece and soy sauce in a skillet for 5-7 minutes until brown.
2. Spread the egg roll wrappers on the working surface and divide the pork filling at the center of the wrappers.
3. Top the pork filling with the coleslaw and wet the edges of each wrapper.
4. Fold the two sides of each roll to cover the filling, and roll each wrapper.
5. Select the "Air Fry" Mode using the Function Keys and select Rack Level 2.
6. Set its cooking time to 7 minutes and temperature to 375 degrees F then press "START/STOP" to initiate preheating.
7. Place all the egg rolls in the Air Fryer basket evenly.
8. Transfer the egg rolls to the Ninja Foodi XL Pro Air Fryer Oven and Close its door.
9. Serve warm.

Serving Suggestion: Serve the egg rolls with tomato ketchup.

Variation Tip: Add grated cheese to the filling to make your egg rolls taste cheesy.

Nutritional Information Per Serving:
Calories 204 | Fat 6.1g | Sodium 216mg | Carbs 17g | Fiber 2g | Sugar 2g | Protein 23g

Avocado Fries

Prep Time: 15 minutes.
Cook Time: 20 minutes.
Serves: 2

Ingredients:

- 1/2 cup panko breadcrumbs
- 1/2 teaspoon salt
- 1 avocado, peeled, pitted, and sliced
- 1 cup egg, whisked

Preparation:

1. Toss breadcrumbs with salt in a shallow bowl.
2. First, dip the avocado strips in the egg, then coat them with panko.
3. Spread these slices in the Air Fryer basket evenly.
4. Transfer the avocado slices to the Ninja XL Pro Air Fry Oven and Close its door.
5. Select the "Bake" Mode using the Function Keys and select Rack Level 2.
6. Set its cooking time to 20 minutes and temperature to 400 degrees F then press "START/STOP" to initiate preheating.
7. Serve fresh.

Serving Suggestion: Serve the fries with mayonnaise dip.

Variation Tip: Ground chicken or beef can also be used instead of ground sausage.

Nutritional Information Per Serving:
Calories 149 | Fat 12g | Sodium 79mg | Carbs 13g | Fiber 1.1g | Sugar 3g | Protein 5g

Ranch Kale Chips

Prep Time: 15 minutes.
Cook Time: 5 minutes.
Serves: 6

Ingredients:

- 2 tablespoons olive oil
- 4 cups kale leaves
- 2 teaspoons Ranch Seasoning
- 1 tablespoon nutritional yeast flakes
- 1/4 teaspoon salt

Preparation:

1. Toss the kale leaves with oil, yeast, and Ranch seasoning in a large bowl.
2. Spread the seasoned kale leaves in the Air Fryer.
3. Transfer the kale leaves to the Ninja XL Pro Air Fry Oven and Close its door.
4. Select the "Air Fry" Mode using the Function Keys and select Rack Level 2.
5. Set its cooking time to 5 minutes and temperature to 370 degrees F then press "START/STOP" to initiate preheating.
6. Serve warm.

Serving Suggestion: Serve the chips with cream cheese dip.

Variation Tip: Add paprika for more spice.

Nutritional Information Per Serving:
Calories 113 | Fat 4g | Sodium 162mg | Carbs 13g | Fiber 2.7g | Sugar 1g | Protein 2g

Cheese Sticks

Prep Time: 15 minutes.
Cook Time: 7 minutes.
Serves: 6

Ingredients:

- 2 eggs, beaten
- ¼ cup of water
- 1 ½ cups Italian seasoned bread crumbs
- ½ teaspoon garlic salt
- ⅔ cup all-purpose flour
- ⅓ cup cornstarch
- 1 (16 ounces) package mozzarella cheese sticks

Preparation:

1. Whisk and beat eggs with water in a shallow bowl and keep it aside.
2. Mix flour with cornstarch and seasonings in another shallow bowl.
3. Coat the mozzarella cheese sticks with flour mixture.
4. Dip the cheese sticks in the eggs and coat with breadcrumbs.
5. Transfer these cheese sticks to the Air Fryer.
6. Place the cheese sticks to the Ninja XL Pro Air Fry Oven and Close its door.
7. Select the "Air Fry" Mode using the Function Keys and select Rack Level 2.
8. Set its cooking time to 7 minutes and temperature to 370 degrees F then press "START/STOP" to initiate preheating.
9. Serve warm.

Serving Suggestion: Serve the sticks with mayo dip.

Variation Tip: Add dried herbs to the breading.

Nutritional Information Per Serving:
Calories 179 | Fat 30g | Sodium 193mg | Carbs 14g | Fiber 0.4g | Sugar 1.3g | Protein 10.2g

Plantains Chips

Prep Time: 15 minutes.
Cook Time: 10 minutes.
Serves: 4

Ingredients:

- 2 ripe plantains, sliced
- 2 teaspoons avocado oil
- 1/8 teaspoons salt

Preparation:

1. Gently toss the plantains with oil and salt in a bowl.
2. Spread them in the Air Fryer basket evenly.
3. Place the plantains in the Ninja XL Pro Air Fry Oven and Close its door.
4. Select the "Air Fry" Mode using the Function Keys and select Rack Level 2.
5. Set its cooking time to 10 minutes and temperature to 400 degrees F then press "START/STOP" to initiate preheating.
6. Flip the plantain chips after 5 minutes and resume cooking.
7. Serve fresh.

Serving Suggestion: Serve the chips with cream cheese dip.

Variation Tip: Add seasoned salt for better taste.

Nutritional Information Per Serving:
Calories 168 | Fat 25g |Sodium 351mg | Carbs 72.3g | Fiber 9.4g | Sugar 9g | Protein 7.2g

Buffalo Cauliflower

Prep Time: 15 minutes.
Cook Time: 25 minutes.
Serves: 4

Ingredients:
- 1 cup all-purpose flour
- 1 teaspoon bouillon granules
- 1/4 teaspoon cayenne pepper
- 1/4 teaspoon chili powder
- 1/4 teaspoon paprika
- 1/4 teaspoon dried chipotle chili flakes
- 1 cup of soy milk
- 1 large head cauliflower, cut into pieces
- Canola oil spray
- 2 tablespoons non-dairy butter
- 1/2 cup cayenne pepper sauce
- 2 garlic cloves, minced

Preparation:
1. Whisk flour with cayenne, chili powder, bouillon granules, chipotle flakes, and paprika in a large bowl.
2. Gradually, pour in milk and mix well until it forms a smooth batter.
3. Add the cauliflower pieces to the flour batter and mix to coat well.
4. Place these cauliflower pieces in the Air Fryer basket and spray them with canola oil.
5. Transfer the sheet to the Ninja XL Pro Air Fry Oven and Close its door.
6. Select the "Air Fry" Mode using the Function Keys and select Rack Level 2.
7. Set its cooking time to 20 minutes and temperature to 390 degrees F then press "START/STOP" to initiate preheating.
8. Flip the cauliflower pieces after 10 minutes and resume cooking.
9. Meanwhile, melt butter in a small-sized saucepan and add garlic and hot sauce.
10. Stir cook this mixture until it thickens.
11. Pour this sauce over the air fried cauliflower and serve warm.

Serving Suggestion: Serve the cauliflower with mayo dip.
Variation Tip: Use hot sauce for more spice.
Nutritional Information Per Serving:
Calories 101 | Fat 25g | Sodium 276mg | Carbs 25g | Fiber 1.4g | Sugar 1.4g | Protein **8.8**g

Potato Fries

Prep Time: 15 minutes.

Cook Time: 14 minutes.

Serves: 4

Ingredients:

- 1 Russet potato, cut into sticks
- 1 tablespoon canola oil
- 1/4 teaspoon sea salt
- 1/4 teaspoon black pepper
- 1 teaspoon chopped fresh rosemary

Preparation:

1. Soak potato fries in cold water for 20 minutes, then drain and pat them dry.
2. Toss the slices with oil, black pepper, salt and rosemary in a bowl.
3. Select the "Air Fry" Mode using the Function Keys and select Rack Level 2.
4. Set its cooking time to 14 minutes and temperature to 380 degrees F then press "START/STOP" to initiate preheating.
5. Evenly spread the potato sticks in the Air fryer basket.
6. Transfer the basket to the Ninja Foodi XL Pro Air Fryer Oven and Close its door.
7. Toss the chips after 10 minutes and resume cooking.
8. Serve.

Serving Suggestion: Serve the chips with tomato ketchup.

Variation Tip: Add paprika for more spice.

Nutritional Information Per Serving:
Calories 155 | Fat 15g |Sodium 332mg | Carbs 22.3g | Fiber 0.4g | Sugar 1g | Protein 6.3g

Sweet Potato Tots

Prep Time: 15 minutes.
Cook Time: 14 minutes.
Serves: 4

Ingredients:

- 2 small sweet potatoes, peeled
- 1 tablespoon potato starch
- 1/8 teaspoon garlic powder
- 1 1/4 teaspoon kosher salt
- 3/4 cup ketchup
- Cooking spray

Preparation:

1. Boil all the sweet potatoes in water for 15 minutes until soft.
2. Drain and transfer to a bowl, then mash well.
3. Stir in garlic powder, salt, ketchup, and potato starch.
4. Mix well until smooth and lump-free.
5. Make 24 (1-inch) sweet potato tots out of this mixture.
6. Place the tots in the air fryer basket and coat with cooking spray.
7. Transfer the tots to the Air Fry Oven.
8. Select the "Air Fry" Mode using the Function Keys and select Rack Level 3.
9. Set its cooking time to 14 minutes and temperature to 400 degrees F then press "START/STOP" to initiate preheating.
10. Toss the tots after 5 minutes and resume cooking.
11. Serve.

Serving Suggestion: Serve the tots with tomato ketchup.

Variation Tip: Add paprika for more spice.

Nutritional Information Per Serving:
Calories 245 | Fat 10g |Sodium 572mg | Carbs 24.3g | Fiber 2.4g | Sugar 4g | Protein 5.1g

Sweet Potato Chips

Prep Time: 15 minutes.
Cook Time: 15 minutes.
Serves: 4

Ingredients:

- 1 medium sweet potato, sliced
- 1 tablespoon canola oil
- 1/4 teaspoon sea salt
- 1/4 teaspoon black pepper
- 1 teaspoon fresh rosemary, chopped

Preparation:

1. Soak sliced sweet potato in cold water for 20 minutes, then drain and pat them dry.
2. Toss the slices with seasoning, oil, and rosemary in a bowl.
3. Evenly spread the sweet potato slices in the Air fryer basket.
4. Transfer the basket to the Ninja XL Pro Air Fry Oven and Close its door.
5. Select the "Air Fry" Mode using the Function Keys and select Rack Level 2.
6. Set its cooking time to 15 minutes and temperature to 350 degrees F then press "START/STOP" to initiate preheating.
7. Toss the chips after 10 minutes and resume cooking.
8. Serve.

Serving Suggestion: Serve the chips with tomato ketchup.

Variation Tip: Add paprika for more spice.

Nutritional Information Per Serving:
Calories 175 | Fat 16g | Sodium 255mg | Carbs 31g | Fiber 1.2g | Sugar 5g | Protein 4.1g

Onion Rings

Prep Time: 15 minutes.
Cook Time: 15 minutes.
Serves: 4

Ingredients:

- 1/2 cup all-purpose flour
- 1 teaspoon smoked paprika
- 1/2 teaspoon kosher salt,
- 1 large egg
- 1 tablespoon water
- 1 cup whole-wheat panko
- 1 (10-ounces) large onion, cut into 1/2-in.-thick rounds
- Cooking spray

Preparation:

1. Whisk flour, paprika, and salt in one bowl beat egg with water in another, and spread the panko in the third bowl.
2. Coat the onion rings with flour, then with egg, and finally with breadcrumbs.
3. Place the rings in the air fryer basket and transfer to the Air Fry Oven.
4. Select the "Air Fry" Mode using the Function Keys and select Rack Level 2.
5. Set its cooking time to 10 minutes and temperature to 375 degrees F then press "START/STOP" to initiate preheating.
6. Flip the rings after 5 minutes and resume cooking.
7. Serve.

Serving Suggestion: Serve the rings with tomato ketchup.

Variation Tip: Add garlic salt for more taste.

Nutritional Information Per Serving:
Calories 251 | Fat 17g |Sodium 723mg | Carbs 21g | Fiber 2.5g | Sugar 2g | Protein 7.3g

Chapter Three: Poultry Recipes

Panko Chicken Breast

Prep Time: 15 minutes.
Cook Time: 15 minutes.
Serves: 2

Ingredients:
- 1 large egg, beaten
- 1/4 cup all-purpose flour
- 3/4 cup panko bread crumbs
- 1/3 cup Parmesan, grated
- 2 teaspoons lemon zest
- 1 teaspoon dried oregano
- 1/2 teaspoon cayenne pepper
- Salt, to taste
- Black pepper, to taste
- 2 chicken breasts, boneless skinless

Preparation:
1. Beat eggs in one bowl and spread the flour in another shallow bowl.
2. Whisk panko with cayenne, salt, black pepper, oregano, lemon zest, and parmesan in a shallow tray.
3. Take 2 chicken breasts and coat them with flour, then dip in eggs.
4. Coat the chicken breasts with the panko mixture and place them in the Air Fryer.
5. Place this Air Fryer basket inside the Ninja XL Pro Air Fry Oven and Close its door.
6. Select the "Air Fry" Mode using the Function Keys and select Rack Level 2.
7. Set its cooking time to 10 minutes and temperature to 350 degrees F then press "START/STOP" to initiate preheating.
8. Flip the chicken and return to cooking for another 5 minutes on the same mode and temperature.
9. Serve warm.

Serving Suggestion: Serve the chicken soaked in white cream sauce.
Variation Tip: Add paprika for more spice.
Nutritional Information Per Serving:
Calories 453 | Fat 2.4g | Sodium 216mg | Carbs 18g | Fiber 2.3g | Sugar 1.2g | Protein 23.2g

Maple Chicken Thighs

Prep Time: 15 minutes.
Cook Time: 25 minutes.
Serves: 4

Ingredients:

- ½ cup maple syrup
- 1 cup buttermilk
- 1 egg
- 1 teaspoon garlic powder
- 4 chicken thighs, skin-on, bone-in

Dry Rub:

- ½ cup all-purpose flour
- ½ teaspoons honey powder
- 1 tablespoon of salt
- 1 teaspoon sweet paprika
- ¼ teaspoons smoked paprika
- 1 teaspoon onion powder
- ¼ teaspoons ground black pepper
- ¼ cup tapioca flour
- ½ teaspoons cayenne pepper
- ½ teaspoons garlic powder

Preparation:

1. Whisk buttermilk, egg, maple syrup, and a teaspoon of garlic in a Ziplock bag.
2. Add the chicken thighs to the buttermilk and seal this bag. Shake it to coat the chicken well, then refrigerator for 1 hour.
3. Meanwhile, whisk the flour with salt, tapioca, pepper, smoked paprika, sweet paprika, honey powder, granulated garlic, cayenne pepper, and granulated onion in a bowl.
4. Remove the marinated chicken from its bag and coat it with the flour mixture.
5. Shake off the excess and place the chicken in the Air Fryer.
6. Place this sheet inside the Ninja XL Pro Air Fry Oven and Close its door.
7. Select the "Air Fry" Mode using the Function Keys and select Rack Level 2.
8. Set its cooking time to 12 minutes and temperature to 380 degrees F then press "START/STOP" to initiate preheating.
9. Flip the chicken thighs and continue baking for another 13 minutes at the same temperature.
10. Serve warm.

Serving Suggestion: Serve the chicken with fresh herbs on top.
Variation Tip: Use honey instead of maple syrup.
Nutritional Information Per Serving:
Calories 529 | Fat 17g |Sodium 391mg | Carbs 55g | Fiber 6g | Sugar 8g | Protein 41g

Chicken Bake

Prep Time: 15 minutes.
Cook Time: 40 minutes.
Serves: 4

Ingredients:

- 1 tablespoon olive oil
- 1 yellow onion, chopped
- 1 can (14 ½ ounces) canned tomatoes, diced
- 3 garlic cloves, minced
- 2 tablespoons fresh parsley, chopped
- 1 teaspoon dried oregano
- 4 boneless chicken breasts
- Salt and black pepper, to taste
- 3/4 cup gruyere cheese, grated
- 1 teaspoon Italian seasoning
- 1 tablespoon parsley, for garnish

Preparation:

1. Grease the Ninja baking dish with cooking spray.
2. Toss the tomatoes with olive oil, garlic, onions, Italian seasoning, oregano, and parsley in a bowl.
3. Spread this tomato mixture in the prepared baking dish.
4. Rub the chicken with salt and black pepper, then place over the tomatoes.
5. Transfer this baking dish to the Ninja XL Pro Air Fry Oven and Close its door.
6. Select the "Air Fry" Mode using the Function Keys and select Rack Level 2.
7. Set its cooking time to 35 minutes and temperature to 400 degrees F then press "START/STOP" to initiate preheating.
8. Drizzle the cheese over the chicken and bake for 5 minutes.
9. Serve warm.

Serving Suggestion: Serve the chicken bake with toasted bread slices.

Variation Tip: Add sliced potatoes to layer the casserole.

Nutritional Information Per Serving:
Calories 297 | Fat 14g | Sodium 364mg | Carbs 8g | Fiber 1g | Sugar 3g | Protein 32g

Crumbed Tenderloins

Prep Time: 15 minutes.
Cook Time: 15 minutes.
Serves: 4

Ingredients:

- 1 egg
- ½ cup dry bread crumbs
- 2 tablespoons vegetable oil
- 8 chicken tenderloins

Preparation:

1. Whisk egg in a bowl and mix crumbs with oil in another bowl.
2. First, dip the chicken in the egg, then coat well with crumbs mixture.
3. Shake off the excess, then place the tenderloins in the Air Fryer.
4. Transfer this sheet to the Ninja XL Pro Air Fry Oven and Close its door.
5. Select the "Air Fry" Mode using the Function Keys and select Rack Level 2.
6. Set its cooking time to 12 minutes and temperature to 350 degrees F then press "START/STOP" to initiate preheating.
7. Serve warm.

Serving Suggestion: Serve the tenderloins with lemon wedges on the side.

Variation Tip: Use crushed cornflakes for crisper.

Nutritional Information Per Serving:
Calories 352 | Fat 14g | Sodium 220mg | Carbs 16g | Fiber 0.2g | Sugar 1g | Protein 26g

Chicken Schnitzel

Prep Time: 15 minutes.
Cook Time: 12 minutes.
Serves: 2

Ingredients:

- 1 lb. chicken thighs, skinless, boneless
- ½ cup seasoned bread crumbs
- 1 teaspoon salt
- ½ teaspoons ground black pepper
- ¼ cup flour
- 1 egg, beaten
- Avocado oil or cooking spray

Preparation:

1. Place one chicken thigh in between 2 sheets of parchment sheet and use a mallet to flatten the chicken.
2. Similarly, flatten the remaining thighs using this method.
3. Now mix bread crumbs with black pepper and salt in a shallow bowl.
4. Spread flour in another bowl and whisk the egg in yet another bowl.
5. First coat the chicken with flour, then dip into the egg.
6. Place the flattened chicken in the crumbs and flip to coat well, then shake off excess.
7. Keep the chicken thighs in the Air Fryer basket.
8. Transfer this Air Fryer basket to the Ninja XL Pro Air Fry Oven and Close its door.
9. Select the "Air Fry" Mode using the Function Keys and select Rack Level 2.
10. Set its cooking time to 6 minutes and temperature to 375 degrees F then press "START/STOP" to initiate preheating.
11. Flip the cooked chicken and continue cooking for another 6 minutes on the same mode and temperature.
12. Serve warm.

Serving Suggestion: Serve the chicken on top of lettuce leaves.

Variation Tip: Use crushed cornflakes for a more crispy texture.

Nutritional Information Per Serving:
Calories 388 | Fat 8g |Sodium 339mg | Carbs 8g | Fiber 1g | Sugar 2g | Protein 13g

Sesame Chicken Thighs

Prep Time: 15 minutes.
Cook Time: 15 minutes.
Serves: 4

Ingredients:

- 2 tablespoons sesame oil
- 2 tablespoons soy sauce
- 1 tablespoon honey
- 1 tablespoon sriracha sauce
- 1 teaspoon rice vinegar
- 2 lbs. chicken thighs
- 1 green onion, chopped
- 2 tablespoons toasted sesame seeds

Preparation:

1. Whisk vinegar, sriracha, honey, soy sauce, and sesame oil in a large bowl.
2. Toss in chicken and mix well to coat it with sriracha sauce.
3. Cover this sriracha-honey chicken and refrigerate for 30 minutes to marinate.
4. Transfer the marinated chicken to the Air Fryer.
5. Place this Air Fryer basket to the Ninja XL Pro Air Fry Oven and Close its door.
6. Select the "Air Fry" Mode using the Function Keys and select Rack Level 2.
7. Set its cooking time to 5 minutes and temperature to 400 degrees F then press "START/STOP" to initiate preheating.
8. Flip the sesame chicken and continue Air frying for another 10 minutes on the same mode and temperature.
9. Garnish with sesame seeds and green onions.
10. Serve warm.

Serving Suggestion: Serve the chicken with toasted bread slices.

Variation Tip: Use tahini for seasoning and marination.

Nutritional Information Per Serving:
Calories 301 | Fat 16g | Sodium 189mg | Carbs 32g | Fiber 0.3g | Sugar 0.1g | Protein 28.2g

Baked Butter Thighs

Prep Time: 15 minutes.
Cook Time: 35 minutes.
Serves: 6

Ingredients:

- Zest of 1 lemon
- Salt, to taste
- 1/2 cup butter
- 1 lb. baby potatoes, quartered
- 5 garlic cloves, minced
- 1 tablespoon fresh thyme leaves
- 1 lemon, cut into rounds
- Black pepper, to taste
- 3 lb. (6) bone-in, skin-on chicken thighs
- 1 tablespoon freshly parsley, chopped

Preparation:

1. Pat dry all the chicken thighs and rub them with salt and black pepper.
2. Whisk butter with lemon zest, thyme, and garlic in a small bowl.
3. Rub this butter thyme mixture over the chicken thighs liberally
4. Place these chicken thighs, potatoes, and lemon rounds in a casserole dish.
5. Transfer the casserole dish to the Ninja XL Pro Air Fry Oven and Close its door.
6. Select the "Bake" Mode using the Function Keys and select Rack Level 2.
7. Set its cooking time to 35 minutes and temperature to 420 degrees F then press "START/STOP" to initiate preheating.
8. Serve warm.

Serving Suggestion: Serve the chicken thighs with Greek salad.

Variation Tip: Add dried herbs for seasoning.

Nutritional Information Per Serving:
Calories 231 | Fat 20g |Sodium 941mg | Carbs 30g | Fiber 0.9g | Sugar 1.4g | Protein 14.6g

Primavera Chicken

Prep Time: 15 minutes.
Cook Time: 25 minutes.
Serves: 4

Ingredients:

- 4 boneless chicken breasts
- 2 tablespoons olive oil
- Salt, to taste
- Black pepper, to taste
- 1 zucchini, sliced
- 3 medium tomatoes, sliced
- 1/2 red onion, sliced
- 1 cup mozzarella, cheese shredded
- 1 teaspoon Italian seasoning
- 2 yellow bell peppers, sliced
- Freshly parsley, for garnish

Preparation:

1. Carve one side slit in the chicken breasts and stuff them with all the veggies.
2. Place these stuffed chicken breasts in a casserole dish, then drizzle oil, Italian seasoning, black pepper, salt, and Mozzarella over the chicken.
3. Place this casserole dish in the Ninja XL Pro Air Fry Oven and Close its door.
4. Select the "Bake" Mode using the Function Keys and select Rack Level 2.
5. Set its cooking time to 25 minutes and temperature to 370 degrees F then press "START/STOP" to initiate preheating.
6. Garnish with parsley and serve warm.

Serving Suggestion: Serve the chicken with a mixed greens salad.

Variation Tip: Use cheese slices to stuff in the slits.

Nutritional Information Per Serving:
Calories 440 | Fat 7.9g |Sodium 581mg | Carbs 21.8g | Fiber 2.6g | Sugar 7g | Protein 37.2g

Chicken Meatballs

Prep Time: 15 minutes.
Cook Time: 13 minutes.
Serves: 8

Ingredients:

- 1 pound chicken mince
- 1 pound mild Italian sausage
- ¼ cup onion, minced
- 2 cloves garlic, minced
- 2 tablespoons parsley, chopped
- 2 eggs
- 1½ cup parmesan cheese, grated
- Salt and black pepper, to taste
- ½ teaspoon crushed red pepper flakes
- ½ teaspoon Italian seasoning

Preparation:

1. Mix chicken mince with sausage, onion, garlic, eggs, parsley, parmesan cheese, black pepper, salt, red pepper and Italian seasoning in a bowl..
2. Make small golf-ball sized balls out of this mixture.
3. Select the "air fry" mode using the Function Keys and select Rack Level 2.
4. Set its cooking time to 13 minutes and temperature to 375 degrees F then press "START/STOP" to initiate preheating.
5. Once preheated, place the meatballs in the Air fryer basket and transfer to the air fryer oven.
6. Close the lid and let the meatballs cook.
7. Serve warm.

Serving Suggestion: Serve the meatballs with tomato sauce and toasted bread slices.

Variation Tip: Roll the meatballs in breadcrumbs before air frying to get a crispy texture.

Nutritional Information Per Serving:
Calories 419 | Fat 13g |Sodium 432mg | Carbs 9.1g | Fiber 3g | Sugar 1g | Protein 33g

Chapter Four: Beef, Pork, and Lamb

Lamb Leg with Mint Sauce

Prep Time: 15 minutes.
Cook Time: 1 hr. 30 minutes.
Serves: 8

Ingredients:

- 4 lbs. leg of lamb
- 1 bulb of garlic, peeled
- ½ a bunch of fresh rosemary
- 1 lemon, juiced
- 1 teaspoon olive oil

Mint Sauce

- 1 bunch of fresh mint
- 1 teaspoon sugar
- 3 tablespoons wine vinegar

Preparation:

1. Rub the lamb with salt and black pepper, then place it in a casserole dish.
2. Toss the remaining ingredients together in a bowl, then spread it around the lamb.
3. Place the lamb dish in the Ninja XL Pro Air Fry Oven and Close its door.
4. Select the "Bake" Mode using the Function Keys and select Rack Level 2.
5. Set its cooking time to 1 hr. 30 minutes and temperature to 400 degrees F then press "START/STOP" to initiate preheating.
6. Meanwhile, prepare the mint sauce by blending all its ingredients in a blender.
7. Serve the lamb with mint sauce on top.
8. Enjoy.

Serving Suggestion: Serve the lamb leg with roasted bell peppers and cherry tomatoes.

Variation Tip: Wrap the lamb leg with a vegetable of your choice in a foil sheet before baking.

Nutritional Information Per Serving:
Calories 380 | Fat 20g |Sodium 686mg | Carbs 33g | Fiber 1g | Sugar 1.2g | Protein 21g

Roast Lamb with Potatoes

Prep Time: 15 minutes.
Cook Time: 60 minutes.
Serves: 6

Ingredients:

- 4 garlic cloves, minced
- 3 tablespoons olive oil
- 1 (2-lb.) boneless lamb shoulder roast
- Salt, to taste
- 1 tablespoon rosemary, chopped
- 2 teaspoons fresh thyme leaves
- Black pepper, to taste
- 2 lb. baby potatoes, halved

Preparation:

1. Whisk garlic, thyme, rosemary, salt, black pepper, and 1 tablespoon oil in a small bowl.
2. Rub this mixture well over the lamb, then place it in a casserole dish.
3. Cover the lamb with potato, then place the dish in the Ninja XL Pro Air Fry Oven and Close its door.
4. Select the "Bake" Mode using the Function Keys and select Rack Level 2.
5. Set its cooking time to 60 minutes and temperature to 370 degrees F then press "START/STOP" to initiate preheating.
6. Slice the roast and serve warm.

Serving Suggestion: Serve the lamb with blue cheese on top.

Variation Tip: Use barbecue sauce for seasoning.

Nutritional Information Per Serving:
Calories 361 | Fat 16g |Sodium 515mg | Carbs 19.3g | Fiber 0.1g | Sugar 18.2g | Protein 33.3g

Lamb Chops with Garlic Sauce

Prep Time: 15 minutes.
Cook Time: 15 minutes.
Serves: 8

Ingredients:

- 1 garlic bulb, peeled
- 3 tablespoons olive oil
- Sea salt, to taste
- Black pepper, to taste
- 1 tablespoon fresh oregano, chopped
- 8 lamb chops

Preparation:

1. Rub lamb chops with oil, oregano, salt, and black pepper.
2. Place 4 of these chops in the casserole dish, then spread the garlic cloves around them.
3. Transfer the chops to the Ninja XL Pro Air Fry Oven and Close its door.
4. Select the "Air Fry" Mode using the Function Keys and select Rack Level 2.
5. Set its cooking time to 10 minutes and temperature to 370 degrees F then press "START/STOP" to initiate preheating.
6. Flip the chops and continue Air frying for another 5 minutes.
7. Cook the remaining four chops following the same steps.
8. Squeeze the baked garlic and mix it with the lamb chops drippings.
9. Serve the chops with garlic mixture on top.
10. Enjoy.

Serving Suggestion: Serve the chops with fresh herbs on top.

Variation Tip: Add butter to the chops before cooking.

Nutritional Information Per Serving:

Calories 405 | Fat 22.7g |Sodium 227mg | Carbs 26.1g | Fiber 1.4g | Sugar 0.9g | Protein 45.2g

Breaded Pork Chops

Prep Time: 15 minutes.
Cook Time: 12 minutes.
Serves: 3

Ingredients:

- 3 (6ounces) pork chops, rinsed
- Salt, to taste
- Black pepper, to taste
- Garlic powder, to taste
- Smoked paprika, to taste
- 1/2 cup breadcrumbs
- 1 large egg

Preparation:

1. First, rub the pork chops with garlic powder, black pepper, salt, and smoked paprika.
2. Spread the breadcrumbs in a shallow bowl and beat the egg in another bowl.
3. Dip each chop in egg first, then coat it well with breadcrumbs.
4. Place these chops in the Air Fryer basket.
5. Transfer these chops to the Ninja XL Pro Air Fry Oven and Close its door.
6. Select the "Air Fry" Mode using the Function Keys and select Rack Level 2.
7. Set its cooking time to 12 minutes and temperature to 380 degrees F then press "START/STOP" to initiate preheating.
8. Flip the chops after 6 minutes and resume cooking.
9. Serve warm.

Serving Suggestion: Serve the chops with fresh greens.

Variation Tip: Use crushed cornflakes for a more crispy texture.

Nutritional Information Per Serving:
Calories 545 | Fat 36g | Sodium 272mg | Carbs 41g | Fiber 0.2g | Sugar 0.1g | Protein 42.5g

Pork Chops with Broccoli

Prep Time: 15 minutes.
Cook Time: 10 minutes.
Serves: 2

Ingredients:

- 2 (5 ounces) bone-in pork chops
- 2 tablespoons avocado oil
- 1/2 teaspoon paprika
- 1/2 teaspoon onion powder
- 1/2 teaspoon garlic powder
- 1 teaspoon salt, divided
- 2 cups broccoli florets
- 2 garlic cloves, minced

Preparation:

1. Rub the chops with half of the oil, salt, garlic powder, onion powder, and paprika liberally.
2. Place these chops in the Air frying sheet of the Ninja XL Pro Air Fry Oven.
3. Toss the broccoli and garlic with remaining oil and salt, then spread them around the pork chops.
4. Transfer the chops and veggies to the Ninja XL Pro Air Fry Oven and Close its door.
5. Select the "Bake" Mode using the Function Keys and select Rack Level 2.
6. Set its cooking time to 5 minutes and temperature to 370 degrees F then press "START/STOP" to initiate preheating.
7. Flip the chops and all the veggies, then continue cooking for another 5 minutes.
8. Serve warm.

Serving Suggestion: Serve the chops with butter cube on top.

Variation Tip: Drizzle parmesan cheese on top before cooking.

Nutritional Information Per Serving:
Calories 395 | Fat 9.5g | Sodium 655mg | Carbs 13.4g | Fiber 0.4g | Sugar 0.4g | Protein 28.3g

Garlicky Pork Chops

Prep Time: 15 minutes.
Cook Time: 35 minutes.
Serves: 4

Ingredients:

- 2 lbs. Yukon gold potatoes, diced
- 3 tablespoons canola oil
- 4 bone-in pork loin chops
- 2 tablespoons garlic minced
- 1/2 cup brown sugar packed
- Salt, to taste
- Ground black pepper, to taste

Preparation:

1. Season the potatoes with oil, salt, black pepper, and spread them in the Air Fry sheet.
2. Now whisk brown sugar with salt and black pepper, then season the pork chops with this sweet mixture.
3. Place these chops in the Air Fryer Basket and transfer to the Ninja XL Pro Air Fry Oven. Close its door.
4. Select the "Bake" Mode using the Function Keys and select Rack Level 2.
5. Set its cooking time to 35 minutes and temperature to 375 degrees F then press "START/STOP" to initiate preheating.
6. Serve warm.

Serving Suggestion: Serve the chops with toasted bread slices.

Variation Tip: Add sweet potatoes or squash instead of potatoes.

Nutritional Information Per Serving:
Calories 301 | Fat 5g |Sodium 340mg | Carbs 24.7g | Fiber 1.2g | Sugar 1.3g | Protein 15.3g

Spiced Pork Chops

Prep Time: 15 minutes.
Cook Time: 18 minutes.
Serves: 4

Ingredients:

- 1 tablespoon paprika
- 2 teaspoons onion powder
- 2 teaspoons garlic powder
- 1 teaspoon oregano
- Salt, to taste
- Black pepper, to taste
- 2 tablespoons olive oil
- 4 boneless pork chops

Preparation:

1. Season the pork with olive oil, salt, oregano, pepper, paprika, garlic powder, and onion powder.
2. Transfer these chops to the cooking pan of the Ninja XL Pro Air Fry Oven and place it in the Ninja XL Pro Air Fry Oven, then close its door.
3. Select the "bake" mode using the Function Keys and select Rack Level 2.
4. Set its cooking time to 18 minutes and temperature to 400 degrees F then press "START/STOP" to initiate preheating.
5. Serve warm.

Serving Suggestion: Serve the chops with roasted veggies.

Variation Tip: Brush with barbecue sauce instead.

Nutritional Information Per Serving:
Calories 548 | Fat 23g | Sodium 350mg | Carbs 18g | Fiber 6.3g | Sugar 1g | Protein 40.3g

Russian Beef

Prep Time: 15 minutes.
Cook Time: 60 minutes.
Serves: 4

Ingredients:

- 1 (2 lbs.) beef tenderloin, sliced
- Salt and black pepper to taste
- 2 onions, sliced
- 1 1/2 cups Cheddar cheese, grated
- 1 cup milk
- 3 tablespoons mayonnaise

Preparation:

1. Slice the beef and season it with salt and black pepper.
2. Place these beef strips in the casserole dish, then add onions, cheddar cheese, milk, and mayonnaise to the beef.
3. Toss well, then transfer this casserole dish to the Ninja XL Pro Air Fry Oven and Close its door.
4. Select the "Bake" Mode using the Function Keys and select Rack Level 2.
5. Set its cooking time to 60 minutes and temperature to 350 degrees F then press "START/STOP" to initiate preheating.
6. Serve warm.

Serving Suggestion: Serve the beef with toasted bread slices.

Variation Tip: Ground chicken or beef can also be used instead of tenderloin.

Nutritional Information Per Serving:
Calories 309 | Fat 25g | Sodium 463mg | Carbs 9.9g | Fiber 0.3g | Sugar 0.3g | Protein 18g

Beef Potato Medley

Prep Time: 15 minutes.
Cook Time: 1 hr. 30 minutes.
Serves: 6

Ingredients:

- 3 tablespoons soy sauce
- 1 tablespoon Worcestershire sauce
- ¼ cup flour
- Salt, to taste
- Black pepper, to taste
- 3 bay leaves
- 3 sprigs thyme
- 2 lbs. lean beef, cubed
- 3 garlic cloves, minced
- 1 carrot, sliced
- 1 onion, sliced
- 6 new potatoes, halved
- 2 celery ribs, sliced
- 1 cup red wine
- 1 cup beef stock
- 2 tablespoons parsley, chopped

Preparation:

1. Whisk soy sauce, seasoning, flour, Worcestershire, thyme, and bay leaves in a casserole dish.
2. Toss in veggies and meat to this mixture and mix well.
3. Finally, pour in red wine and beef stock, then give it a gentle stir.
4. Cover this casserole dish with a foil sheet and poke two-three holes in it.
5. Transfer this casserole dish to the Ninja XL Pro Air Fry Oven and Close its door.
6. Select the "Bake" Mode using the Function Keys and select Rack Level 2.
7. Set its cooking time to 1 hr. 30 minutes and temperature to 350 degrees F then press "START/STOP" to initiate preheating.
8. Serve warm.

Serving Suggestion: Serve the medley with tortilla slices.
Variation Tip: Ground beef can also be used instead.
Nutritional Information Per Serving:
Calories 537 | Fat 20g | Sodium 719mg | Carbs 25.1g | Fiber 0.9g | Sugar 1.4g | Protein 37.8g

Chapter Five: Seafood Recipes

Baked Shrimp with Garlic Sauce

Prep Time: 15 minutes.
Cook Time: 9 minutes.
Serves: 4

Ingredients:

- 1/4 cup butter
- 1 tablespoon garlic, minced
- 2 tablespoons fresh lemon juice
- Salt and black pepper, to taste
- 1/8 teaspoons red pepper flakes
- 1 ¼ lbs large shrimp, peeled and deveined
- 2 tablespoons fresh parsley, minced

Preparation:

1. Spread the shrimp in the Ninja foodi baking dish.
2. Melt butter in a pan and sauté garlic in it for 30 seconds.
3. Stir in lemon, then pour this mixture over the shrimp.
4. Drizzle salt, black pepper, and red pepper flakes over the shrimp.
5. Gently toss the shrimp, then transfer this dish to Ninja XL Pro Air Fry Oven and Close its door.
6. Select the "Bake" Mode using the Function Keys and select Rack Level 2.
7. Set its cooking time to 9 minutes and temperature to 300 degrees F then press "START/STOP" to initiate preheating.
8. Serve warm.

Serving Suggestion: Serve the shrimp on top of the risotto.

Variation Tip: Add paprika for more spice.

Nutritional Information Per Serving:
Calories 248 | Fat 13g | Sodium 353mg | Carbs 1g | Fiber 0.4g | Sugar 1g | Protein 29g

Haddock Cream Casserole

Prep Time: 15 minutes.
Cook Time: 20 minutes.
Serves: 8

Ingredients:

- 8 oz haddock, skinned and diced
- 1 lb scallops
- 1 lb large shrimp, peeled and deveined
- 3 garlic cloves, minced
- 1/2 cup heavy cream
- 1/2 cup Swiss cheese, shredded
- 2 tablespoons Parmesan, grated
- Paprika, to taste
- Sea salt and black pepper, to taste

Preparation:

1. Toss shrimp, scallops, and haddock chunks in the Ninja baking dish greased with cooking spray.
2. Drizzle salt, black pepper, and minced garlic over the seafood mix.
3. Top this seafood with cream, Swiss cheese, paprika, and Parmesan cheese.
4. Transfer the dish to the Ninja XL Pro Air Fry Oven and Close its door.
5. Select the "Bake" Mode using the Function Keys and select Rack Level 2.
6. Set its cooking time to 20 minutes and temperature to 375 degrees F then press "START/STOP" to initiate preheating.
7. Serve warm.

Serving Suggestion: Serve the casserole with toasted bread slices.

Variation Tip: Drizzle breadcrumbs on top for a crispy touch.

Nutritional Information Per Serving:
Calories 457 | Fat 19g | Sodium 557mg | Carbs 19g | Fiber 1.8g | Sugar 1.2g | Protein 32.5g

Halibut Scallops Bake

Prep Time: 15 minutes.
Cook Time: 12 minutes.
Serves: 8

Ingredients:

- 2 (4 ounces) halibut fillets, cubed
- 6 scallops
- 6 shrimp, peeled and deveined
- 1/3 cup dry white wine
- 2 tablespoons melted butter
- 1 tablespoon lemon juice
- 1/2 teaspoon Old Bay seasoning
- 1 teaspoon garlic, minced
- Salt and pepper to taste
- 1 tablespoon fresh parsley, chopped

Preparation:

1. Toss halibut chunks, shrimp, and scallops in the Ninja baking dish.
2. Whisk wine, lemon juice, and butter in a small bowl and pour over the seafood.
3. Drizzle seasoning, garlic, salt, and black pepper over the seafood mixture.
4. Transfer the baking dish to the Ninja XL Pro Air Fry Oven and Close its door.
5. Select the "bake" mode using the Function Keys and select Rack Level 2.
6. Set its cooking time to 12 minutes and temperature to 450 degrees F then press "START/STOP" to initiate preheating.
7. Garnish with parsley.
8. Serve warm.

Serving Suggestion: Serve the baked seafood with alfredo sauce on top.

Variation Tip: Marinate the seasoned seafood for 20 minutes.

Nutritional Information Per Serving:
Calories 392 | Fat 16g | Sodium 466mg | Carbs 3.9g | Fiber 0.9g | Sugar 0.6g | Protein 48g

Dill Seafood Paella

Prep Time: 15 minutes.
Cook Time: 30 minutes.
Serves: 8

Ingredients:

- 1 cup unsalted butter melted
- 3 tablespoons fresh dill, chopped
- 2 tablespoons garlic minced
- Salt, to taste
- Black pepper, to taste
- 24 ounces baby red potato
- 4 fillets cod,
- 30 shrimp raw, peeled, and deveined
- 8 lemon slices
- 4 corn ears, husked and halved

Preparation:

1. Cut the foil sheet into 8- 2 feet squares and place 4 pieces over a working surface.
2. Place the remaining pieces over these pieces to double them.
3. Spray each group of foil sheets with cooking oil to grease them.
4. Now melt butter in a glass bowl and add baby dill, black pepper, salt, and garlic.
5. Mix well and keep this dill butter aside.
6. Place each fish fillet over one square of greased foil, then top it with 6 shrimp, 2 corn halves, ½ cup potatoes, and ¼ of the dill butter.
7. Finally, set 2 lemon slices on top of each fillet and wrap each foil sheet around the toppings.
8. Place the fish pockets inside the Ninja XL Pro Air Fry Oven ad Close its door.
9. Select the "bake" mode using the Function Keys and select Rack Level 2.
10. Set its cooking time to 30 minutes and temperature to 350 degrees F then press "START/STOP" to initiate preheating.
11. Unwrap the baked fish and serve warm with the veggies.
12. Enjoy.

Serving Suggestion: Serve the seafood mix with fried rice.
Variation Tip: Add boiled rice or noodles to the mixture.
Nutritional Information Per Serving:
Calories 321 | Fat 7.4g |Sodium 356mg | Carbs 22.3g | Fiber 2.4g | Sugar 5g | Protein 37.2g

Lobster Tail Casserole

Prep Time: 15 minutes.
Cook Time: 16 minutes.
Serves: 6

Ingredients:

- 2 tablespoons fresh tarragon, chopped
- 1 lb. salmon fillets, cut into 8 equal pieces
- 16 large sea scallops
- 16 large prawns, peeled and deveined
- 1/2 teaspoon paprika
- 8 lobster tails, meat only, cubed
- 1/3 cup butter
- 1/4 cup white wine
- 1/4 cup lemon juice
- 2 medium garlic cloves, minced
- 1/4 teaspoon ground cayenne pepper

Preparation:

1. Whisk butter with lemon juice, wine, garlic, tarragon, paprika, salt, and cayenne pepper in a small saucepan.
2. Stir cook this mixture over medium heat for 1 minute.
3. Toss the seafood in the Ninja baking dish and pour the butter mixture on top.
4. Transfer this baking dish to the Ninja XL Pro Air Fry Oven and Close its door.
5. Select the "bake" mode using the Function Keys and select Rack Level 2.
6. Set its cooking time to 15 minutes and temperature to 450 degrees F then press "START/STOP" to initiate preheating.
7. Serve warm.

Serving Suggestion: Serve the casserole with toasted bread slices.

Variation Tip: Add crab roe and peas to the casserole.

Nutritional Information Per Serving:
Calories 248 | Fat 16g |Sodium 94mg | Carbs 31.4g | Fiber 0.4g | Sugar 3g | Protein 24.9g

Breaded Shrimp

Prep Time: 15 minutes.
Cook Time: 4 minutes.
Serves: 4

Ingredients:

- 1 lb. raw shrimp peeled and deveined
- 1 egg white
- 1/2 cup all-purpose flour
- 3/4 cup panko bread crumbs
- 1 teaspoon paprika
- Montreal Chicken Seasoning to taste
- Salt and pepper to taste
- Cooking spray

Bang Bang Sauce

- 1/3 cup plain Greek yogurt
- 2 tablespoons Sriracha
- 1/4 cup sweet chili sauce

Preparation:

1. Spread flour in one bowl, beat the egg in another, and breadcrumbs in a shallow tray.
2. Season the shrimp with paprika, Montreal seasoning, salt, and black pepper.
3. First coat the shrimp with flour, then dip in the egg and coat with breadcrumbs.
4. Place the shrimps in the Air Fryer basket and spray them with cooking oil.
5. Transfer the Air Fryer basket to the Ninja XL Pro Air Fry Oven and close its door.
6. Select the "bake" mode using the Function Keys and select Rack Level 2.
7. Set its cooking time to 4 minutes and temperature to 400 degrees F then press "START/STOP" to initiate preheating.
8. Meanwhile, mix the yogurt, sriracha, and sweet chili sauce in a bowl.
9. Serve the air fried shrimp with bang bang sauce.
10. Enjoy.

Serving Suggestion: Serve the shrimp with ketchup.
Variation Tip: Use white pepper for a change of flavor.
Nutritional Information Per Serving:
Calories 378 | Fat 21g |Sodium 146mg | Carbs 7.1g | Fiber 0.1g | Sugar 0.4g | Protein 23g

Garlic Parmesan Shrimp

Prep Time: 15 minutes.
Cook Time: 10 minutes.
Serves: 4

Ingredients:

- 1 lb. shrimp, deveined and peeled
- 1 tablespoon olive oil
- 1 teaspoon salt
- 1 teaspoon fresh cracked pepper
- 1 tablespoon lemon juice
- 6 garlic cloves, diced
- ½ cup parmesan cheese, grated

Preparation:

1. Toss the shrimp with olive oil, lemon juice, salt, garlic, and black pepper in a large bowl.
2. Cover the shrimp and refrigerate for 3 hours.
3. Add parmesan cheese to the shrimp and toss it gently to coat.
4. Spread the shrimp over the Air Fryer basket and transfer to the Ninja XL Pro Air Fry Oven, then close its door.
5. Select the "bake" mode using the Function Keys and select Rack Level 2.
6. Set its cooking time to 10 minutes and temperature to 350 degrees F then press "START/STOP" to initiate preheating.
7. Serve warm.

Serving Suggestion: Serve the shrimp with crusted fish and boiled eggs.

Variation Tip: Drizzle cheddar cheese on top for a rich taste.

Nutritional Information Per Serving:
Calories 351 | Fat 4g |Sodium 236mg | Carbs 19.1g | Fiber 0.3g | Sugar 0.1g | Protein 36g

White Fish with Lemon Pepper

Prep Time: 15 minutes.
Cook Time: 12 minutes.
Serves: 2

Ingredients:

- 2 (6 ounces) tilapia filets
- 1/2 teaspoon garlic powder
- 1/2 teaspoon lemon pepper seasoning
- 1/2 teaspoon onion powder
- Salt, to taste
- Black pepper, to taste
- Fresh chopped parsley
- Lemon wedges

Preparation:

1. Rub the tilapia fillets with olive oil, garlic powder, onion powder, lemon pepper, salt, and black pepper liberally.
2. Place the seasoned fish fillets on the Air Fryer.
3. Transfer this Air Fryer basket to the Ninja XL Pro Air Fry Oven and Close its door.
4. Select the "Air Fry" Mode using the Function Keys and select Rack Level 2.
5. Set its cooking time to 12 minutes and temperature to 360 degrees F then press "START/STOP" to initiate preheating.
6. Garnish with parsley and lemon wedges.
7. Serve warm.

Serving Suggestion: Serve the fish with mashed potatoes.

Variation Tip: Add dried herbs to the coating.

Nutritional Information Per Serving:
Calories 378 | Fat 7g | Sodium 316mg | Carbs 16.2g | Fiber 0.3g | Sugar 0.3g | Protein 26g

Seafood Mushrooms Casserole

Prep Time: 15 minutes.
Cook Time: 25 minutes.
Serves: 8

Ingredients:

- 5 tablespoons butter
- 4 ounces mushrooms, sliced
- 16 ounces shrimp
- 8 ounces of lobster meat, diced
- 4 ounces crabmeat, diced
- 1/4 cup flour
- 2 cups of milk
- Salt, to taste
- Black pepper, to taste
- 1/4 teaspoon paprika
- 2 teaspoons chives, snipped
- 2 teaspoons parsley, chopped
- 2 tablespoons dry white wine
- 4 tablespoons Parmesan cheese

Preparation:

1. Sauté mushroom with 1 tablespoon butter in a pan until soft.
2. Grease a casserole dish with butter, then add seafood and mushrooms.
3. Melt rest of the butter in a suitable saucepan, then add flour.
4. Stir and cook for 2 minutes, then pour in milk with continuous stirring.
5. Cook until it bubbles, then add wine, herbs, and seasonings.
6. Pour this sauce over the seafood and top it with cheese.
7. Transfer the seafood casserole to the Air Fry Oven.
8. Select the "bake" mode using the Function Keys and select Rack Level 2.
9. Set its cooking time to 20 minutes and temperature to 350 degrees F then press "START/STOP" to initiate preheating.
10. Serve immediately.

Serving Suggestion: Serve the casserole with toasted bread slices.
Variation Tip: Add chopped veggies and mushrooms.
Nutritional Information Per Serving:
Calories 415 | Fat 15g | Sodium 634mg | Carbs 14.3g | Fiber 1.4g | Sugar 1g | Protein 23.3g

Chapter Six: Vegetables and Sides

Italian Baked Vegetables

Prep Time: 15 minutes.
Cook Time: 15 minutes.
Serves: 4

Ingredients:

- 2 bell peppers cored, chopped
- 2 carrots, peeled and sliced
- 1 zucchini, ends trimmed, sliced
- 1 broccoli, florets
- ½ red onion, peeled and diced
- 2 tablespoons olive oil
- 1 ½ teaspoon Italian seasoning
- 2 garlic cloves, minced
- Salt and Black pepper, to taste
- 1 cup grape tomatoes
- 1 tablespoon fresh lemon juice

Preparation:

1. Toss all the veggies with olive oil, Italian seasoning, salt, black pepper, and garlic in a large salad bowl.
2. Spread this broccoli-zucchini mixture in the Ninja baking pan.
3. Transfer the baking pan to the Ninja XL Pro Air Fry Oven and close its door.
4. Select the "bake" mode using the Function Keys and select Rack Level 2.
5. Set its cooking time to 15 minutes and temperature to 400 degrees F then press "START/STOP" to initiate preheating.
6. Serve warm with lemon juice on top.
7. Enjoy.

Serving Suggestion: Serve the veggies as a pizza topping.

Variation Tip: Add olives or sliced mushrooms.

Nutritional Information Per Serving:
Calories 246 | Fat 15g | Sodium 220mg | Carbs 40.3g | Fiber 2.4g | Sugar 1.2g | Protein 12.4g

Vegetable Casserole

Prep Time: 15 minutes.
Cook Time: 45 minutes.
Serves: 6

Ingredients:

- 2 cups peas
- 8 ounces mushrooms, sliced
- 4 tablespoons all-purpose flour
- 1 ½ cups celery, sliced
- 1 ½ cups carrots, sliced
- ½ teaspoon mustard powder
- 2 cups of milk

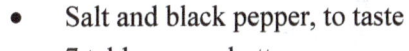

- Salt and black pepper, to taste
- 7 tablespoons butter
- 1 cup breadcrumbs
- ½ cup Parmesan cheese, grated

Preparation:

1. Grease and rub a casserole dish with butter and keep it aside.
2. Add carrots, onion, and celery to a saucepan, then fill it with water.
3. Cover this pot and cook for 10 minutes, then stir in peas.
4. Cook for 4 minutes, then strain the vegetables.
5. Now melt 1 tablespoon butter in the same saucepan and toss in mushrooms to sauté.
6. Once the mushrooms are soft, transfer them to the vegetables.
7. Prepare the sauce by melting 4 tablespoons butter in a saucepan.
8. Stir in mustard and flour, then stir cook for 2 minutes.
9. Gradually pour in the milk and stir cook until thickened, then add salt and black pepper.
10. Add vegetables and mushrooms to the flour milk mixture and mix well to blend.
11. Spread this vegetable blend in the casserole dish evenly.
12. Toss the breadcrumbs with the remaining butter and spread it on top of the vegetables.
13. Top this casserole dish with cheese.
14. Transfer the vegetable casserole to the Ninja XL Pro Air Fry Oven and close its door.
15. Select the "bake" mode using the Function Keys and select Rack Level 2.
16. Set its cooking time to 25 minutes and temperature to 350 degrees F then press "START/STOP" to initiate preheating.
17. Serve warm.

Serving Suggestion: Serve the casserole with toasted bread slices.
Variation Tip: Add toasted croutons on top.
Nutritional Information Per Serving:
Calories 338 | Fat 24g | Sodium 620mg | Carbs 58.3g | Fiber 2.4g | Sugar 1.2g | Protein 5.4g

Sweet Potato Casserole

Prep Time: 15 minutes.
Cook Time: 35 minutes.
Serves: 8

Ingredients:

- 3 cups brown sugar, packed
- 1 ½ cup butter, melted
- 4 large eggs, beaten
- 2 teaspoons vanilla extract
- 1 cup milk
- 6 cups sweet potatoes, boiled and mashed
- 2/3 cup flour
- 8 ounces pecans, chopped

Preparation:

1. Mix the sweet potato mash with vanilla extract, milk, eggs, 2 ½ brown sugar, and 1 cup melted butter in a large bowl.
2. Spread this sweet potato mixture in a casserole dish.
3. Now whisk remaining sugar and butter with flour in a separate bowl.
4. Fold in pecan, then top the sweet potatoes mixed with this pecan mixture.
5. Transfer the sweet potato casserole to the Ninja XL Pro Air Fry Oven and close its door.
6. Select the "bake" mode using the Function Keys and select Rack Level 2.
7. Set its cooking time to 35 minutes and temperature to 350 degrees F then press "START/STOP" to initiate preheating.
8. Slice and serve!

Serving Suggestion: Serve the casserole with toasted bread slices.

Variation Tip: Ground chicken or beef can also be used instead of ground sausage.

Nutritional Information Per Serving:
Calories 421 | Fat 10.1g | Sodium 380mg | Carbs 25.3g | Fiber 2.4g | Sugar 1.2g | Protein 2.1g

Brussels Sprouts Gratin

Prep Time: 15 minutes.
Cook Time: 30 minutes.
Serves: 8

Ingredients:

- 1 lb. Brussels sprouts
- 1 garlic clove, cut in half
- 3 tablespoons butter, divided
- 2 tablespoons shallots, minced
- 2 tablespoons all-purpose flour
- Salt, to taste
- Black pepper
- 1 dash ground nutmeg

- 1 cup milk
- 1/2 cup fontina cheese, shredded
- 1 strip of bacon, cooked and crumbled
- 1/2 cup fine bread crumbs

Preparation:

1. Trim the Brussels sprouts and remove their outer leaves.
2. Slice the sprouts into quarters, then rinse them under cold water.
3. Grease a gratin dish with cooking spray and rub it with garlic halves.
4. Boil salted water in a suitable pan, then add Brussels sprouts.
5. Cook the sprouts for 3 minutes, then immediately drain.
6. Place a suitable saucepan over medium-low heat and melt 2 tablespoons butter in it.
7. Toss in shallots and sauté until soft, then stir in flour, nutmeg, ½ teaspoons salt, and black pepper.
8. Stir cook for 2 minutes, then gradually add milk and a half and half cream.
9. Mix well and add bacon along with shredded cheese.
10. Fold in brussels sprouts and transfer this mixture to the casserole dish.
11. Toss breadcrumbs with 1 tablespoon butter and spread over the casserole.
12. Transfer the Brussels sprouts casserole to the Ninja XL Pro Air Fry Oven and close its door.
13. Select the "bake" mode using the Function Keys and select Rack Level 2.
14. Set its cooking time to 25 minutes and temperature to 350 degrees F then press "START/STOP" to initiate preheating.
15. Enjoy!

Serving Suggestion: Serve the gratin with toasted bread slices.
Variation Tip: Use crushed cornflakes for a more crispy texture.
Nutritional Information Per Serving:
Calories 378 | Fat 3.8g |Sodium 620mg | Carbs 13.3g | Fiber 2.4g | Sugar 1.2g | Protein 5.4g

Green Bean Casserole

Prep Time: 15 minutes.
Cook Time: 25 minutes.
Serves: 6

Ingredients:

- 4 cups green beans, cooked and chopped
- 3 tablespoons butter
- 8 ounces mushrooms, sliced
- ¼ cup onion, chopped
- 2 tablespoons flour
- 1 teaspoon salt
- ¼ teaspoon ground black pepper
- 1 ½ cups milk
- 2 cups cheddar cheese, shredded
- 2 tablespoons sour cream
- 1 cup soft breadcrumbs
- 2 tablespoons butter, melted
- ¼ cup Parmesan cheese, grated
- 1 cup French fried onions

Preparation:

1. Add butter to a suitable saucepan and melt it over medium-low heat.
2. Toss in onion and mushrooms, then sauté until soft.
3. Stir in flour, salt, and black. Mix well, then slowly pour in the milk.
4. Stir in sour cream, green beans, and cheddar cheese, then cook until it thickens.
5. Transfer this green bean mixture to a casserole dish and spread it evenly.
6. Toss breadcrumbs with fried onion and butter.
7. Top the casserole with this breadcrumb's mixture.
8. Transfer the vegetable cream casserole to the Ninja XL Pro Air Fry Oven and close its door.
9. Select the "bake" mode using the Function Keys and select Rack Level 2.
10. Set its cooking time to 25 minutes and temperature to 350 degrees F then press "START/STOP" to initiate preheating.
11. Serve and enjoy!

Serving Suggestion: Serve the casserole with mashed potatoes.

Variation Tip: Add crispy dried onion for better taste.

Nutritional Information Per Serving:
Calories 304 | Fat 31g | Sodium 834mg | Carbs 21.4g | Fiber 0.2g | Sugar 0.3g | Protein 4.6g

Mayo Broccoli Casserole

Prep Time: 15 minutes.
Cook Time: 45 minutes.
Serves: 6

Ingredients:

- 1 cup mayonnaise
- 10 ½ ounces cream of celery soup
- 2 large eggs, beaten
- 20 ounces broccoli, chopped
- 2 tablespoons onion, minced
- 1 cup Cheddar cheese, grated
- 1 tablespoon Worcestershire sauce
- 1 teaspoon seasoned salt
- Black pepper, to taste
- 2 tablespoons butter

Preparation:

1. Whisk mayonnaise with eggs, condensed soup in a large bowl.
2. Stir in salt, black pepper, Worcestershire sauce, and cheddar cheese.
3. Spread broccoli and onion in a greased casserole dish.
4. Top the veggies with the mayonnaise mixture.
5. Transfer this broccoli casserole to the Ninja XL Pro Air Fry Oven and Close its door.
6. Select the "bake" mode using the Function Keys and select Rack Level 2.
7. Set its cooking time to 45 minutes and temperature to 350 degrees F then press "START/STOP" to initiate preheating.
8. Slice and serve warm.

Serving Suggestion: Serve the casserole with toasted bread slices.

Variation Tip: Add chopped celery sticks to the mixture.

Nutritional Information Per Serving:
Calories 341 | Fat 4g | Sodium 547mg | Carbs 36.4g | Fiber 1.2g | Sugar 1g | Protein 10.3g

Cauliflower Broccoli Medley

Prep Time: 15 minutes.
Cook Time: 8 minutes.
Serves: 2

Ingredients:

- 1/2 lb. broccoli, florets
- 1/2 lb. cauliflower, florets
- 1 tablespoon olive oil
- Black pepper, to taste
- Salt, to taste

Preparation:

1. Toss all the veggies with seasoning in a large bowl.
2. Spread these vegetables in the Air Fryer basket.
3. Place the veggies inside the Ninja XL Pro Air Fry Oven and close its door.
4. Select the "Air Fry" Mode using the Function Keys and select Rack Level 2.
5. Set its cooking time to 8 minutes and temperature to 400 degrees F then press "START/STOP" to initiate preheating.
6. Serve warm.

Serving Suggestion: Serve the veggies with spaghetti squash.

Variation Tip: Add paprika for more spice.

Nutritional Information Per Serving:
Calories 118 | Fat 5.7g |Sodium 124mg | Carbs 7g | Fiber 0.1g | Sugar 0.3g | Protein 4.9g

Vegetables Mix

Prep Time: 15 minutes.
Cook Time: 20 minutes.
Serves: 6

Ingredients:

- 4 ounces mushrooms, sliced
- 1 yellow summer squash, sliced
- 1 zucchini, sliced
- 1 red bell pepper, seeded and sliced
- 1/2 sweet onion, sliced
- 1 tablespoon olive oil
- Salt and black pepper to taste

Preparation:

1. Toss the red bell pepper, zucchini, summer squash, mushrooms, and onion in a large bowl.
2. Stir in black pepper, salt, and olive oil to season the veggies.
3. Spread these vegetables in a baking pan evenly.
4. Transfer these veggies to the Ninja XL Pro Air Fry Oven and close its door.
5. Select the "Bake" Mode using the Function Keys and select Rack Level 2.
6. Set its cooking time to 10 minutes and temperature to 350 degrees F then press "START/STOP" to initiate preheating.
7. Serve warm.

Serving Suggestion: Serve the veggies with boiled rice and tomato sauce.

Variation Tip: Add crushed tomatoes for a saucy texture.

Nutritional Information Per Serving:
Calories 191 | Fat 2.2g |Sodium 276mg | Carbs 7.7g | Fiber 0.9g | Sugar 1.4g | Protein 8.8g

Mushroom Skewers

Prep Time: 15 minutes.
Cook Time: 7 minutes.
Serves: 6

Ingredients:

- 1/4 cup balsamic vinegar
- 2 tablespoons soy sauce
- 2 garlic cloves, minced
- Black pepper
- 1 lb. cremini mushrooms, sliced 1/2" thick

Preparation:

1. Toss mushrooms with vinegar, soy sauce, garlic, and black pepper.
2. Thread them on the mini wooden skewers.
3. Set the skewers in the baking tray and transfer to the Air Fry Oven.
4. Select the "Air Fry" Mode using the Function Keys and select Rack Level 2.
5. Set its cooking time to 7 minutes and temperature to 350 degrees F then press "START/STOP" to initiate preheating.
6. Serve warm.

Serving Suggestion: Serve the mushrooms with barbecue sauce.

Variation Tip: Add paprika for more spice.

Nutritional Information Per Serving:
Calories 324 | Fat 5g | Sodium 432mg | Carbs 13.1g | Fiber 0.3g | Sugar 1g | Protein 5.7g

Chapter Seven: Entertaining Recipes

Chicken Sheet Bake

Prep Time: 15 minutes.
Cook Time: 40 minutes.
Serves: **8**

Ingredients:

- ¼ cup olive oil
- 1 teaspoon fine grind sea salt
- ½ teaspoons pepper
- 12 ounces red potatoes
- 2 medium zucchinis, sliced
- 1 medium yellow squash, sliced
- 1 red onion, sliced
- 1 bulb garlic, chopped

- 16 ounces chicken breast
- 8 sprigs rosemary fresh
- 3 lemons, sliced

Preparation:

1. Slice the red potatoes into quarters and place them in a baking tray.
2. Drizzle black pepper, salt, and olive oil on top.
3. Set the potatoes in the Ninja XL Pro Air Fry Oven and close the lid.
4. Select the "Air Fry" Mode using the Function Keys and select Rack Level 2.
5. Set its cooking time to 10 minutes and temperature to 450 degrees F then press "START/STOP" to initiate preheating.
6. Rub the chicken breast with black pepper, salt, and add to the potatoes.
7. Spread zucchini, squash, and onion around the chicken.
8. Place the lemon slices, garlic, and rosemary on top.
9. Return the baking tray to the Air Fry Oven.
10. Select the "Air Fry" Mode using the Function Keys and select Rack Level 2.
11. Set its cooking time to 30 minutes and temperature to 325 degrees F then press "START/STOP" to initiate preheating.
12. Serve warm.

Serving Suggestion: Serve the chicken with toasted bread slices.
Variation Tip: Add corn kernels to the mixture.
Nutritional Information Per Serving:
Calories 305 | Fat 25g |Sodium 532mg | Carbs 2.3g | Fiber 0.4g | Sugar 2g | Protein 18.3g

Chicken Enchiladas

Prep Time: 15 minutes.
Cook Time: 6 minutes.
Serves: 12

Ingredients:

- 12 corn tortillas
- 1½ cups Mexican Chicken, Shredded
- 2 cups Enchilada Sauce
- 1½ cups Mexican Cheese, Shredded

Preparation:

1. Place six corn tortillas in the air fryer basket at a time.
2. Spray cooking oil on top and set the basket in the Ninja XL Pro Air Fry Oven.
3. Select the "Air Fry" Mode using the Function Keys and select Rack Level 2.
4. Set its cooking time to 3 minutes and temperature to 3425 degrees F then press "START/STOP" to initiate preheating.
5. Divide the shredded chicken and enchiladas sauce in each tortilla.
6. Set the prepared tortillas in a baking tray and drizzle shredded cheese on top.
7. Slide this tray into the Air Fry Oven and close its door.
8. Select the "Broil" Mode using the Function Keys and select Rack Level 2.
9. Set its cooking time to 3 minutes and temperature to 325 degrees F then press "START/STOP" to initiate preheating.
10. Serve warm.

Serving Suggestion: Serve the casserole with toasted bread slices.

Variation Tip: Add cream cheese and pepperoni slices.

Nutritional Information Per Serving:
Calories 305 | Fat 25g | Sodium 532mg | Carbs 2.3g | Fiber 0.4g | Sugar 2g | Protein 18.3g

Roasted Chicken

Prep Time: 15 minutes.
Cook Time: 50 minutes.
Serves: 10

Ingredients:

- 1 (5 lb.) whole chicken, giblets removed
- 2 tablespoons avocado oil
- 1 tablespoon kosher salt
- 1 teaspoon black pepper
- 1 teaspoon garlic powder
- 1 teaspoon paprika
- 1/2 teaspoon dried basil
- 1/2 teaspoon dried oregano
- 1/2 teaspoon dried thyme

Preparation:

1. Rub the chicken with avocado oil, salt, black pepper, garlic powder, paprika, basil, oregano, and thyme.
2. Place the seasoned chicken in a baking tray.
3. Set the baking tray in the Ninja XL Pro Air Fry Oven and close its door.
4. Select the "Whole Roast" Mode using the Function Keys and select Rack Level 2.
5. Set its cooking time to 50 minutes and temperature to 360 degrees F then press "START/STOP" to initiate preheating.
6. Flip the whole chicken and cook for another 10 minutes.
7. Serve warm.

Serving Suggestion: Serve the chicken with roasted veggies.

Variation Tip: Stuff the chicken with garlic, onion, and celery.

Nutritional Information Per Serving:
Calories 305 | Fat 25g | Sodium 532mg | Carbs 2.3g | Fiber 0.4g | Sugar 2g | Protein 18.3g

Whole Turkey with Gravy

Prep Time: 15 minutes.
Cook Time: 2 hrs. 30 minutes.
Serves: 20

Ingredients:

- 14 lb. raw Whole Turkey
- 6 tablespoons butter, cut into slices
- 4 garlic cloves, sliced thin
- 1 tablespoon kosher salt, or to taste
- Black pepper, to taste
- Oil to coat turkey
- 1 ½ cups chicken broth
- 3/4 cup flour

Preparation:

1. Mix butter with garlic and stuff it under the turkey skin.
2. Rub salt, black pepper, and oil over turkey.
3. Place the seasoned turkey in the baking tray and pour ½ cup broth on top.
4. Set the tray in the Ninja XL Pro Air Fry Oven and close its door.
5. Select the "Whole Roast" mode using the Function Keys and select Rack Level 2.
6. Set its cooking time to 2 hrs. 30 minutes and temperature to 350 degrees F then press "START/STOP" to initiate preheating.
7. And baste the turkey after every 30 minutes.
8. Then transfer the roasted turkey to a serving plate and cover it with a foil sheet.
9. Pour the turkey cooking juices into a saucepan, add remaining broth and other ingredients.
10. Set the pan over medium heat and cook until it thickens.
11. Pour this sauce over the roasted turkey.
12. Serve warm.

Serving Suggestion: Serve the turkey with fresh lemon juice and herbs on top.

Variation Tip: Stuff the turkey with oranges, lemon, garlic, and onion.

Nutritional Information Per Serving:
Calories 305 | Fat 25g | Sodium 532mg | Carbs 2.3g | Fiber 0.4g | Sugar 2g | Protein 18.3g

Turkey breast

Prep Time: 15 minutes.
Cook Time: 60 minutes.
Serves: 6

Ingredients:

- 3 lbs. boneless breast
- ¼ cup mayonnaise
- 2 teaspoons poultry seasoning
- 1 teaspoon salt
- ½ teaspoons garlic powder
- ¼ teaspoons black pepper

Preparation:

1. Mix mayonnaise, poultry seasoning, black pepper, garlic powder, and salt in a bowl.
2. Rub this mixture over the turkey breast and set in a baking tray.
3. Set this baking tray in the Ninja XL Pro Air Fry Oven.
4. Select the "Air Fry" Mode using the Function Keys and select Rack Level 2.
5. Set its cooking time to 60 minutes and temperature to 360 degrees F then press "START/STOP" to initiate preheating.
6. Flip the turkey once cooked halfway through.
7. Serve warm.

Serving Suggestion: Serve the turkey with a maple glaze on top.

Variation Tip: Brush with barbecue sauce before cooking.

Nutritional Information Per Serving:
Calories 305 | Fat 25g |Sodium 532mg | Carbs 2.3g | Fiber 0.4g | Sugar 2g | Protein 18.3g

Baked Potatoes

Prep Time: 15 minutes.
Cook Time: 45 minutes.
Serves: 6

Ingredients:

- 6 large russet potatoes, scrubbed
- 1 tablespoon olive oil
- Kosher salt, to taste
- 1/2 cup butter, softened
- 1/2 cup milk
- 1/2 cup sour cream
- 1 1/2 cup Cheddar cheese, shredded
- 2 green onions, thinly sliced
- Black pepper, to taste

Preparation:

1. Score the potatoes with a fork and rub with salt and oil.
2. Place the potatoes in a baking tray and transfer to the Air Fry Oven.
3. Select the "bake" mode using the Function Keys and select Rack Level 2.
4. Set its cooking time to 40 minutes and temperature to 400 degrees F then press "START/STOP" to initiate preheating.
5. Cut the potatoes from the top lengthwise to make a slit and scoop out some flesh from the center.
6. Add potato flesh, sour cream, milk, and butter to a bowl, then mix well.
7. Stir in green onions, black pepper, salt, and 1 cup cheese, then mix well.
8. Divide and stuff this mixture in the potato slits.
9. Set them in the air fryer basket and place them in the Ninja XL Pro Air Fry Oven.
10. Select the "bake" mode using the Function Keys and select Rack Level 2.
11. Set its cooking time to 5 minutes and temperature to 400 degrees F then press "START/STOP" to initiate preheating.
12. Garnish with green onions.
13. Serve warm.

Serving Suggestion: Serve the potatoes with roasted green beans and cream dip.

Variation Tip: Add crumbled bacon or cooked ground meat to the filling.

Nutritional Information Per Serving:
Calories 305 | Fat 25g |Sodium 532mg | Carbs 2.3g | Fiber 0.4g | Sugar 2g | Protein 18.3g

Air Fried Pizza

Prep Time: 15 minutes.
Cook Time: 12 minutes.
Serves: 6

Ingredients:

- 1 (8-ounces) package pizza dough
- ½ tablespoons olive oil
- 1/4 cup crushed tomatoes
- ½ garlic clove, minced
- 1/4 teaspoon oregano
- Kosher salt, to taste
- Black pepper, to taste
- 1/4 (8-ounces) mozzarella ball, cut into ¼" slices
- Basil leaves, for serving

Preparation:

1. Spread the pizza dough into an 8-inch pizza pan.
2. Brush it with olive oil, and top it with tomatoes.
3. Drizzle garlic, oregano, salt, black pepper, and Mozzarella on top.
4. Set the pizza in the Ninja XL Pro Air Fry Oven.
5. Select the "Pizza" Mode using the Function Keys and select Rack Level 2.
6. Set its cooking time to 12 minutes and temperature to 400 degrees F then press "START/STOP" to initiate preheating.
7. Serve warm.

Serving Suggestion: Serve the pizza with tomato ketchup or hot sauce.

Variation Tip: Add sliced jalapenos on top.

Nutritional Information Per Serving:
Calories 305 | Fat 25g | Sodium 532mg | Carbs 2.3g | Fiber 0.4g | Sugar 2g | Protein 18.3g

Blooming Onion

Prep Time: 15 minutes.
Cook Time: 25 minutes.
Serves: 2

Ingredients:

Onion

- 1 large yellow onion
- 3 large eggs
- 1 cup breadcrumbs
- 2 teaspoons paprika
- 1 teaspoon garlic powder
- 1 teaspoon onion powder
- 1 teaspoon kosher salt
- 3 tablespoons olive oil

Sauce

- 2/3 cup mayonnaise
- 2 tablespoons. ketchup
- 1 teaspoon horseradish
- 1/2 teaspoon paprika
- 1/2 teaspoon garlic powder
- 1/4 teaspoon dried oregano
- Kosher salt, to taste

Preparation:

1. Slice the onion from top to bottom vertically into 16 sections while keeping the bottom intact.
2. Whisk eggs with 1 tablespoon water in one bowl and mix breadcrumbs with spices in another bowl.
3. Dip the onion in the egg wash and coat with the breadcrumbs.
4. Place the onion in the air fryer basket and spray with cooking oil on top.
5. Set the air fryer basket in the Ninja XL Pro Air Fry Oven.
6. Select the "Air Fry" Mode using the Function Keys and select Rack Level 2.
7. Set its cooking time to 25 minutes and temperature to 375 degrees F then press "START/STOP" to initiate preheating.

8. Mix mayonnaise, horseradish, ketchup, garlic powder, dried oregano, salt, and paprika in a bowl.
9. Serve the onion with the sauce.
10. Enjoy.

Serving Suggestion: Serve the onion with ketchup or hot sauce.

Variation Tip: Use crushed cornflakes for a more crispy texture.

Nutritional Information Per Serving:
Calories 305 | Fat 25g |Sodium 532mg | Carbs 2.3g | Fiber 0.4g | Sugar 2g | Protein 18.3g

Thanksgiving Turkey

Prep Time: 15 minutes.
Cook Time: 35 minutes.
Serves: 4

Ingredients:

- 1 (2-lbs.) turkey breast
- Kosher salt, to taste
- Black pepper, to taste
- 1 teaspoon thyme, chopped
- 1 teaspoon rosemary, chopped
- 1 teaspoon sage, chopped
- 1/4 cup maple syrup
- 2 tablespoons Dijon mustard
- 1 tablespoon. butter, melted

Preparation:

1. Rub the turkey breast with maple syrup, Dijon mustard, butter, black pepper, and herbs.
2. Place the turkey in a baking tray and set it in the Ninja XL Pro Air Fry Oven.
3. Select the "Air fry" Mode using the Function Keys and select Rack Level 2.
4. Set its cooking time to 35 minutes and temperature to 390 degrees F then press "START/STOP" to initiate preheating.
5. Serve warm.

Serving Suggestion: Serve the turkey with mashed potatoes.

Variation Tip: Use cranberry preserve to season the turkey.

Nutritional Information Per Serving:
Calories 305 | Fat 25g |Sodium 532mg | Carbs 2.3g | Fiber 0.4g | Sugar 2g | Protein 18.3g

Chicken Casserole

Prep Time: 15 minutes.
Cook Time: 65 minutes.
Serves: 8

Ingredients:

- 1/4 teaspoon salt
- 1/2 teaspoon sugar
- 3 dashes black pepper
- 1 tablespoon Ranch dressing
- ¼ cup heavy whipping cream
- 2 medium potatoes, peeled and diced
- 8 oz. boneless chicken breast, cut into cubes
- 2 bacon strips, cut into pieces
- 4 tablespoons unsalted butter, cut into small pieces
- 1 cup cheddar cheese, shredded
- 1 stalk scallion, green part only, sliced

Preparation:

1. Beat ranch dressing, pepper, salt, and sugar in a bowl.
2. Grease a 9x9 inch baking pan and layer with potatoes and chicken.
3. Spread butter, bacon, cheese, scallions, and ranch mixture on top.
4. Cover with a foil sheet and place in the Ninja XL Pro Air Fry Oven.
5. Select the "bake" mode using the Function Keys and select Rack Level 2.
6. Set its cooking time to 45 minutes and temperature to 350 degrees F then press "START/STOP" to initiate preheating.
7. Remove the foil sheet and bake for another 20 minutes in the Ninja XL Pro Air Fry Oven.
8. Serve warm.

Serving Suggestion: Serve the casserole with toasted bread slices.

Variation Tip: Add boiled pasta to the chicken casserole.

Nutritional Information Per Serving:
Calories 305 | Fat 25g | Sodium 532mg | Carbs 2.3g | Fiber 0.4g | Sugar 2g | Protein 18.3g

Fiesta Chicken Casserole

Prep Time: 15 minutes.
Cook Time: 30 minutes.
Serves: 8

Ingredients:

- 4 cups cubed chicken, cooked
- 1 (10- ounce) can Rotel tomatoes
- 1 cup instant rice, uncooked
- 2 cups grated Colby Jack cheese
- 1 (10 1/3 ounce) can Cream of Chicken Soup
- 2 tablespoons taco seasoning
- 2 tablespoons milk
- 1/2 cup canned corn, drained
- 1/2 cup black beans, drained
- Cilantro, chopped

Preparation:

1. Toss chicken with cheese, taco seasoning, corn, black beans, milk, and chicken soup in a bowl.
2. Spread it in a 9x9 inches baking dish, greased with cooking spray.
3. Cover it with a foil sheet and place it in the Ninja XL Pro Air Fry Oven.
4. Select the "bake" mode using the Function Keys and select Rack Level 2.
5. Set its cooking time to 30 minutes and temperature to 390 degrees F then press "START/STOP" to initiate preheating.
6. Serve warm.

Serving Suggestion: Serve the casserole with a tortilla.

Variation Tip: Add canned chickpeas to the casserole.

Nutritional Information Per Serving:
Calories 305 | Fat 25g |Sodium 532mg | Carbs 2.3g | Fiber 0.4g | Sugar 2g | Protein 18.3g

Hash brown casserole

Prep Time: 15 minutes.
Cook Time: 35 minutes.
Serves: 8

Ingredients:

- 3 cups cauliflower, cooked and chopped
- 4 cups frozen potatoes, shredded
- 1 (10 ½ oz) can reduced-fat cream of chicken
- 1 ½ cups plain nonfat Greek yogurt
- 1 onion, diced
- Salt and black pepper to taste
- ¼ cup of sharp cheese. shredded
- 1 cup sharp cheese, shredded

Preparation:

1. Mix cauliflower with potato shreds, cream of chicken, salt, black pepper, ¼ cup cheese, onion, and yogurt in a bowl.
2. Spread this mixture in a 9x13 inches casserole dish and top it with remaining cheese.
3. Set this dish in the Ninja XL Pro Air Fry Oven.
4. Select the "bake" mode using the Function Keys and select Rack Level 2.
5. Set its cooking time to 35 minutes and temperature to 320 degrees F then press "START/STOP" to initiate preheating.
6. Serve warm.

Serving Suggestion: Serve the casserole with toasted bread slices.

Variation Tip: Add crumbled bacon on top.

Nutritional Information Per Serving:
Calories 305 | Fat 25g |Sodium 532mg | Carbs 2.3g | Fiber 0.4g | Sugar 2g | Protein 18.3g

Meatball Casserole

Prep Time: 15 minutes.
Cook Time: 35 minutes.
Serves: 8

Ingredients:

- 1-pound ground beef
- 1/2 cup mozzarella cheese, shredded
- 1/4 cup Parmesan cheese, shredded
- 1 large egg
- 1/2 cup onion, chopped
- 1 teaspoon garlic powder
- 1/2 teaspoon Italian seasoning
- 1/4 teaspoon salt
- 1/2 teaspoon black pepper
- 24 ounces pasta sauce
- 1/3 cup mozzarella cheese, shredded

Preparation:

1. Mix beef with onion, garlic powder, egg, parmesan, Italian seasoning, black pepper, and salt in a bowl.
2. Make golf-ball sized meatballs out of this mixture and spread them in a casserole dish.
3. Set the dish in the Ninja XL Pro Air Fry Oven to bake the meatballs.
4. Select the "bake" mode using the Function Keys and select Rack Level 2.
5. Set its cooking time to 20 minutes and temperature to 400 degrees F then press "START/STOP" to initiate preheating.
6. Top the baked meatballs with the pasta sauce and mozzarella cheese.
7. Bake again for 15 minutes in the Ninja XL Pro Air Fry Oven.
8. Serve warm.

Serving Suggestion: Serve the meatball casserole with boiled spaghetti.

Variation Tip: Add toasted croutons on top.

Nutritional Information Per Serving:
Calories 305 | Fat 25g | Sodium 532mg | Carbs 2.3g | Fiber 0.4g | Sugar 2g | Protein 18.3g

Ground Beef Casserole

Prep Time: 15 minutes.
Cook Time: 35 minutes.
Serves: 8

Ingredients:

- 1 tablespoon vegetable oil
- 1/2 cup red onions, diced
- 2 teaspoons garlic, minced
- 1/2 cup red bell peppers, diced
- 1 lb. ground beef
- 1 tablespoon Worcestershire sauce
- 14 ½ ounces petite tomatoes, diced
- 6 oz tomato paste
- ½ teaspoon onion powder
- ½ teaspoon garlic powder
- 2 1/8 teaspoons seasoning salt

Shredded Cheese

- 1 cup Colby jack cheese, shredded
- 1 cup sharp cheese, shredded
- 1 3/4 cup mozzarella, shredded

Preparation:

1. Sauté onions and bell peppers with vegetable oil in a skillet for 2 minutes.
2. Add garlic and sauté for 20 seconds, then add ground beef.
3. Sauté until brown, then add tomatoes, tomato paste, Worcestershire sauce, garlic powder, salt, and onion powder, then mix well.
4. Transfer this beef mixture to a casserole dish, and top it with cheese.
5. Place the dish in the Ninja XL Pro Air Fry Oven.
6. Select the "bake" mode using the Function Keys and select Rack Level 2.
7. Set its cooking time to 30 minutes and temperature to 350 degrees F then press "START/STOP" to initiate preheating.
8. Serve warm.

Serving Suggestion: Serve the casserole with toasted bread slices.

Variation Tip: Add peas and corns to the casserole.

Nutritional Information Per Serving:
Calories 305 | Fat 25g | Sodium 532mg | Carbs 2.3g | Fiber 0.4g | Sugar 2g | Protein 18.3g

Chapter Eight: Dessert Recipes

Pear Pies

Prep Time: 15 minutes.
Cook Time: 14 minutes.
Serves: 8

Ingredients:
- 4 tablespoons butter
- 6 tablespoons brown sugar
- 1 teaspoon ground cinnamon
- 2 medium pears, peeled and diced
- 1 teaspoon cornstarch
- 2 teaspoons cold water
- 9-inch double-crust pie
- Cooking spray

- ½ tablespoon grapeseed oil
- ¼ cup powdered sugar
- 1 teaspoon milk

Preparation:
1. Sauté pears with butter, cinnamon, and brown sugar in a skillet for 5 minutes.
2. Whisk cornstarch with cold water and pour it into the egg mixture.
3. Stir and cook this mixture for 1 minute until it thickens.
4. Spread the pie crust on a floured surface and cut the dough into 8 rectangles.
5. Divide the filling on top of all the rectangles, then fold in half.
6. Crimp the edges with a fork and cut 4 slits on top.
7. Place the pear pies in the air fryer basket and brush them with grapeseed oil.
8. Set the Air fryer basket in the Ninja XL Pro Air Fry Oven.
9. Select the "bake" mode using the Function Keys and select Rack Level 2.
10. Set its cooking time to 8 minutes and temperature to 385 degrees F then press "START/STOP" to initiate preheating.
11. Mix sugar with milk in a small bowl and brush this mixture on top.
12. Serve.

Serving Suggestion: Serve the pies with mixed fruit jam.
Variation Tip: Add peaches to the fillings.
Nutritional Information Per Serving:
Calories 318 | Fat 20g |Sodium 192mg | Carbs 23.7g | Fiber 0.9g | Sugar 19g | Protein 5.2g

Chocolate Cake

Prep Time: 15 minutes.
Cook Time: 15 minutes.
Serves: 8

Ingredients:

- ¼ cup white sugar
- 3 ½ tablespoons butter, softened
- 1 egg
- 1 tablespoon apricot jam
- 6 tablespoons all-purpose flour
- 1 tablespoon cocoa powder
- Cooking spray
- Salt to taste
- Heavy cream, to serve

Preparation:

1. Beat butter, sugar, egg, and jam in a bowl until creamy.
2. Stir in cocoa powder, salt, and flour, then mix until smooth.
3. Spread this batter in a greased fluted tube pan.
4. Place this pan in the Ninja XL Pro Air Fry Oven and close the lid.
5. Select the "bake" mode using the Function Keys and select Rack Level 2.
6. Set its cooking time to 15 minutes and temperature to 325 degrees F then press "START/STOP" to initiate preheating.
7. Allow the cake to cool, then slice.
8. Garnish with cream.
9. Serve.

Serving Suggestion: Serve the cakes with sprinkles and cream on top.

Variation Tip: Add chopped nuts to the batter.

Nutritional Information Per Serving:
Calories 248 | Fat 16g | Sodium 95mg | Carbs 38.4g | Fiber 0.3g | Sugar 10g | Protein 14.1g

Apple Pies

Prep Time: 15 minutes.
Cook Time: 7 minutes.
Serves: 10

Ingredients:

- 1 (14 ounces) package refrigerated pie crusts
- 1 (21 ounces) can apple pie filling
- 1 egg, beaten
- 2 tablespoons cinnamon sugar
- Cooking spray

Preparation:

1. Spread each pie crust on a lightly floured surface and cut ten 2 ¼ inches circles out of each using a cookie cutter to get 20 circles in total.
2. Divide the apple pie filling into the top 10 circles.
3. Top the filling with the remaining circles on top and crimp the edges with a fork.
4. Brush the pies with beaten eggs and drizzle cinnamon sugar on top.
5. Set the pies in the Air fryer basket and set the basket in the Ninja XL Pro Air Fry Oven.
6. Select the "bake" mode using the Function Keys and select Rack Level 2.
7. Set its cooking time to 7 minutes and temperature to 360 degrees F then press "START/STOP" to initiate preheating.
8. Serve.

Serving Suggestion: Serve the pies with apple sauce.

Variation Tip: Add apple sauce to the filling.

Nutritional Information Per Serving:
Calories 317 | Fat 12g |Sodium 79mg | Carbs 14.8g | Fiber 1.1g | Sugar 8g | Protein 5g

Cherry Crumble

Prep Time: 15 minutes.
Cook Time: 25 minutes.
Serves: 8

Ingredients:

- ⅓ cup butter, crumbled
- 3 cups pitted cherries
- 10 tablespoons white sugar
- 2 teaspoons lemon juice
- 1 cup all-purpose baking flour
- 1 teaspoon vanilla powder
- 1 teaspoon ground nutmeg
- 1 teaspoon ground cinnamon

Preparation:

1. Toss pitted cherries with lemon juice and 2 tablespoons sugar in a bowl.
2. Spread the cherries mixture in an 8 inches baking dish.
3. Whisk flour, butter, and 6 tablespoons sugar in a bowl.
4. Spread this flour mixture on top of the cherries.
5. Mix vanilla powder, nutmeg, cinnamon, and 2 tablespoons sugar in a bowl
6. Drizzle this cinnamon mixture on top of the flour mixture.
7. Select the "bake" mode using the Function Keys and select Rack Level 2.
8. Set its cooking time to 25 minutes and temperature to 325 degrees F then press "START/STOP" to initiate preheating.
9. Serve.

Serving Suggestion: Serve the crumble with fresh berries on top.

Variation Tip: Add blueberry preserves to the filling.

Nutritional Information Per Serving:
Calories 295 | Fat 3g | Sodium 355mg | Carbs 10g | Fiber 1g | Sugar 5g | Protein 1g

Butter Cake

Prep Time: 15 minutes.
Cook Time: 15 minutes.
Serves: 6

Ingredients:

- 7 tablespoons butter
- ¼ cup brown sugar
- 2 tablespoons white sugar
- 1 egg
- 1 ⅔ cups all-purpose flour
- 1 pinch salt
- Cooking spray
- 6 tablespoons milk

Preparation:

1. Grease a fluted tube pan with cooking oil or spray.
2. Beat brown sugar, sugar with butter in a bowl using an electric mixer.
3. Stir in salt, milk, and flour, then mix until smooth.
4. Pour the chocolate batter into a greased tube pan and place it in the Ninja XL Pro Air Fry Oven.
5. Select the "Bake" Mode using the Function Keys and select Rack Level 2.
6. Set its cooking time to 15 minutes and temperature to 350 degrees F then press "START/STOP" to initiate preheating.
7. Allow the baked cake to cool and then remove from the pan.
8. Slice and serve.

Serving Suggestion: Serve the cake with chocolate syrup on top.

Variation Tip: Add vanilla extracts to the batter.

Nutritional Information Per Serving:
Calories 253 | Fat 8.9g | Sodium 340mg | Carbs 24.7g | Fiber 1.2g | Sugar 11.3g | Protein 5.3g

Cherry Eggrolls

Prep Time: 15 minutes.
Cook Time: 5 minutes.
Serves: 8

Ingredients:

- ½ 8 ounces package cream cheese, softened
- ⅓ cup cherry jam
- ¼ cup dried red cherries, chopped
- 16 wonton wrappers
- 1 tablespoon butter, melted
- 3 tablespoons sugar
- ½ teaspoon ground cinnamon

Preparation:

1. Beat cream cheese and cherry jam in a bowl.
2. Stir in dried cherries and refrigerate the mixture for 30 minutes.
3. Spread the wonton wrappers on the working surface.
4. Wet the edges of the wrappers with water.
5. Add a teaspoon of cherry mixture at the center of the wrapper.
6. Fold the two sides of each wrapper and roll these wraps.
7. Place the rolls in the Air fryer basket, spray with cooking oil.
8. Set the basket in the Ninja XL Pro Air Fry Oven and close the lid.
9. Select the "Air Fry" Mode using the Function Keys and select Rack Level 2.
10. Set its cooking time to 5 minutes and temperature to 360 degrees F then press "START/STOP" to initiate preheating.
11. Drizzle cinnamon and sugar on top and serve.

Serving Suggestion: Serve the rolls with sweet cream cheese dip.

Variation Tip: Use strawberry jam instead of cherry jam.

Nutritional Information Per Serving:
Calories 327 | Fat 31g |Sodium 86mg | Carbs 49g | Fiber 1.8g | Sugar 12g | Protein 13.5g

Pecan Apples

Prep Time: 15 minutes.
Cook Time: 15 minutes.
Serves: 4

Ingredients:

- 2 medium apples, top cut and cored
- 1 tablespoon butter, melted
- 2 tablespoons pecans, chopped
- 1 tablespoon brown sugar
- 1 teaspoon all-purpose flour
- ¼ teaspoon apple pie spice
- Vanilla ice cream or yogurt

Preparation:

1. Mix pecans, butter, brown sugar, apple pie spices, and flour in a small bowl.
2. Place the apple in the Air fryer basket, and stuff pecans mixture in it, then place the cut top to cover.
3. Return the basket to the Air Fry Oven.
4. Select the "Air Fry" Mode using the Function Keys and select Rack Level 2.
5. Set its cooking time to 15 minutes and temperature to 360 degrees F then press "START/STOP" to initiate preheating.
6. Serve.

Serving Suggestion: Serve with caramel sauce or chocolate syrup on top.

Variation Tip: Add walnuts to the filling.

Nutritional Information Per Serving:
Calories 398 | Fat 14g |Sodium 272mg | Carbs 34g | Fiber 1g | Sugar 9.3g | Protein 1.3g

Fudgy Brownies

Prep Time: 15 minutes.
Cook Time: 35 minutes.
Serves: 8

Ingredients:

- ¾ cup butter salted
- 1¾ cup dark chocolate chips
- 1 teaspoon espresso powder
- ¾ teaspoons sea salt
- 1½ cups sugar
- 5 large eggs
- ⅓ cup vegetable oil

- 2 teaspoons vanilla extract
- ½ cup unsweetened cocoa powder
- 1½ cups all-purpose flour

Preparation:

1. Add melted butter and 1 cup chocolate chips to a bowl and heat for 2 minutes in the microwave until melted.
2. Mix well, then add 1 teaspoon espresso powder, then stir well.
3. Beat eggs, sugar, salt, vanilla extract, oil, and chocolate mixture in a bowl for 5 seconds.
4. Stir in cocoa powder and flour, then mix until smooth.
5. Add ¾ chocolate chips, then mix with a spatula.
6. Layer an 11 ½ x 9 inches baking pan with parchment pan.
7. Spread the prepared batter in the pan and place it in the Ninja XL Pro Air Fry Oven.
8. Select the "Bake" Mode using the Function Keys and select Rack Level 2.
9. Set its cooking time to 35 minutes and temperature to 325 degrees F then press "START/STOP" to initiate preheating.
10. Allow the cake to cool, then slice.
11. Serve.

Serving Suggestion: Serve the brownies with a scoop of ice cream.

Variation Tip: Add chopped nuts to the batter.

Nutritional Information Per Serving:
Calories 271 | Fat 15g |Sodium 108mg | Carbs 33g | Fiber 1g | Sugar 26g | Protein 4g

Strawberry Roll Cake

Prep Time: 15 minutes.
Cook Time: 12 minutes.
Serves: 6

Ingredients:

Sponge Cake
- ½ cup of sugar
- 4 large eggs
- ¾ cup all-purpose flour
- 1 teaspoon vanilla extract

Filling:
- ½ cup heavy whipping cream
- 1 cup butter salted
- 1 cup confectioner sugar
- 2 teaspoons vanilla extract
- 8 ounces strawberry preserves

Preparation:
1. Beat sugar with 4 eggs in a mixing bowl with an electric mixer for 5 minutes.
2. Stir in vanilla and flour, then mix until smooth.
3. Spread this sponge cake batter in a 13x13 baking pan, lined with parchment paper.
4. Place the cake pan in the Ninja XL Pro Air Fry Oven and close its door.
5. Select the "Bake" Mode using the Function Keys and select Rack Level 2.
6. Set its cooking time to 12 minutes and temperature to 325 degrees F then press "START/STOP" to initiate preheating.
7. Meanwhile, beat cream with butter, vanilla, and sugar in a bowl on medium-high speed until smooth.
8. Place the sponge cake along with the parchment paper on the working surface, top it with buttercream.
9. Add strawberry preserves on top evenly, then roll the cake gently.
10. Slice and serve.

Serving Suggestion: Serve the cake slices with strawberry sauce or jam.
Variation Tip: Use blueberry or cranberry preserve for a change of flavor
Nutritional Information Per Serving:
Calories 245 | Fat 14g |Sodium 122mg | Carbs 23.3g | Fiber 1.2g | Sugar 12g | Protein 4.3g

Conclusion

Ninja Foodi XL Pro Air Fry Oven combines all the necessary cooking operations of the day in a single unit. That has not only brought ease to the kitchen floors but also guaranteed the smart management of kitchen space. Its efficient cooking mechanism has helped professionals as well as homemakers to enhance their cooking skills. If you want to cook like expert chefs and enjoy super crispy and freshly roasted or baked meals in just a snitch, then give Ninja Foodi XL Pro Air Fry Oven a chance.

The big size of this Ninja Foodi XL Pro Air Fry Oven will solve all your cooking problems because there is nothing that this cooking unit can not cook. All you need to do is to add food of different variety according to the recipes shared in this book, set up the cooking mode, cooking time, and temperature, then wait for the beep and Voila! You will be surprised to see the results. From good texture to great taste, now you enjoy it all using your Ninja XL Pro Air Fry Oven. Before the 10 in 1 Ninja XL, I had used several other Air Fry Ovens, and none of them seemed perfect for me since I needed a unit that would offer all the cooking modes, a large capacity, along with an effective heating mechanism. But when I came across the Ninja XL pro, it offered everything that I was looking for. Creating a new menu using this appliance was less of an effort and more fun because it is so user-friendly and easy to use. The multi-level cooking provides even heat through its smart convection mechanism.

So, if you are planning to enjoy all the perks offered by this amazing appliance, then it's about time that you bring it home, set up it on your kitchen counter, and start creating some magical flavors at home. You will be amazed to know how quickly this single cooking unit changes everything in the kitchen for you. No other appliance can make cooking as convenient as the Ninja XL Pro Air Fry Oven. So, try all the air fry oven recipes from this cookbook and create a menu of your own.